WORKING WITH
GROUPS IN THE
WORKPLACE

CONFRONTING
S E X U A L
HARASSMENT

LOUISE YOLTON EBERHARDT

WORKING WITH
GROUPS IN THE
WORKPLACE

CONFRONTING
S E X U A L
HARASSMENT

LOUISE YOLTON EBERHARDT

WHOLE PERSON ASSOCIATES
Duluth, Minnesota

Library of Congress Cataloging in Publication Data 94-61705
ISBN 1-57025-046-4

REPRODUCTION POLICY

Printed in the United States of America

10   9   8   7   6   5   4   3   2   1

WHOLE PERSON ASSOCIATES
210 West Michigan
Duluth MN 55802-1908
800-247-6789

CONTENTS

INTRODUCTION

Before 1980 we had no term for behavior now labeled "sexual harass-ment," and not until the Anita Hill-Clarence Thomas hearings did sexual harassment gain the attention it deserves. In both the workplace and the home, women have experienced sexual harassment for generations. According to the National Council for Research on Women, 50 to 80 percent of American women encounter some type of sexual harassment during their working or academic life.

Simply stated, sexual harassment is the effort by some men, whether consciously or unconsciously, to "put women back in their place"—to remind them they are not equal to men. Sexual harassment attempts to make the victim feel intellectually, emotionally, and professionally infe-rior to the perpetrator. It is most prevalent in the workplace, where many men—who more and more must compete with women for jobs—attempt to keep the playing field of career advancement an uneven surface. More women enter the workplace each day, and experts predict that by the year 2000, 62 percent of all women will work full time—compared to 75 percent of all men. Sexual harassment is often the reaction of men who feel their careers are threatened by the women with whom they now must compete.

We see harassment not only in overtly sexual comments but also in seemingly innocent comments that belittle women. For instance, a man losing a work-related argument may try to shift the momentum his way (and off the subject) by starting a sentence with something like "Well, my dear, if you had the experience I've had . . ." Women should feel equal to men in the workplace and should be treated with respect and equality. The underlying message harassing men send to their victims is "We may not be able to keep you in the kitchen anymore, but we can still talk and act any way we want to around you."

Of course, men can also be the victims of sexual harassment. Of those that are, many experience harassment while in predominately female organiza-tions or divisions. (Still, the overwhelming majority of sexual harassment victims are women, and this book focuses on reeducating both genders to eliminate the harassment of women.)

Harassment also occurs in some workplaces because many organizational leaders and managers allow it or even participate in it themselves—a very dangerous posture for them to take today. The costs to organizations who allow sexual harassment to occur is very high: loss of productivity, lower morale, and high legal fees and court settlements.

Women and men experience sexual harassment very differently and from distinct perspectives. The problem has its roots in gender role socialization and has resulted in outdated behavior patterns—socialization has not caught up with the increased number of women in the workplace. The problem of sexual harassment is linked to sexism and the inherent power it gives men. Many men treat women who are not relatives as sex objects. They have had little or no experience with women as friends, colleagues, or supervisors. Sexual harassment is in many ways a man's refusal or inability to see women as colleagues. Men often do not perceive their behavior as abnormal or wrong—they are simply acting out how they have learned to behave.

Sexual harassment is not really about sex. It is about power gained through control and intimidation—the power experienced by forcing someone to date or have sex with you, the feeling of superiority felt when embarrassing or humiliating another person, the power gained by unnerving someone to the point that they can't do their job or compete successfully.

Victims of sexual harassment experience serious personal and professional costs. They may lose mobility and freedom, develop stress-related illness, be forced to change careers, or even lose their jobs and livelihood. Harassment impacts victims' decisions—consciously or unconsciously—about what they wear or don't wear, where they go, how they sit and walk, where and how they informally network, and how they behave around men and women in general.

Women can experience harassment in the workplace no matter what position they hold. It affects executives and professionals, but even more incidents are reported by secretaries, assistants, trainees, and students. Women in nontraditional jobs face even more severe and constant harassment and women of color are particularly vulnerable, often experiencing a combination of racism and sexism.

After conducting many sexual harassment workshops, several things are clear to me: many women do not want to take it any more and want to find ways to confront sexual violence and harassment, and some men want to act as allies to stop harassment and sexism. Women do not appreciate sexual harassment on the job and want the same freedom to do their jobs their male colleagues enjoy. Contrary to some beliefs, women do not accuse men of sexual harassment to gain an advantage or to hurt men or gain power. Most women, in fact do not tell anyone about their sexual harassment experiences and try to put it out of their own minds. They usually only speak up as a last attempt to end the harassment.

The goal of most sexual harassment training is to change the way men and women relate at work. This training needs to be presented in the larger context of gender discrimination. The training must not only cover the law but should also help participants examine some of their fundamental attitudes about women and men, explore what is wrong in treating women as objects rather than as professionals, and motivate them to share power equally. Because sexual harassment is learned behavior, it can be unlearned.

Although change in this area does not come quickly, sexual harassment training can help improve the organizational climate. All employees need training, not just managers and supervisors, but managers must be well prepared to communicate clearly their support of a harassment-free workplace and to demonstrate this in their behavior when dealing with the issue.

This book is designed to help explore sexual harassment—look at the underlying causes, understand the law and the legal implications, examine the impact, motivate men to become allies, and empower women to speak up. It includes a variety of exercises, some geared to managers and supervisors, others to employees in general, and a few tailored specifically for women. Some exercises require more sharing and openness than others, so take time to choose those that will work for your particular group. The activities can be used in companies, government agencies, schools, religious institutions, and nonprofit organizations, including women's groups.

Reeducating men and women to become more aware of and to change their attitudes about sexual harassment is difficult work, and a great deal of care needs to be employed when conducting exercises and workshops. Do not use these exercises without first reading "Sexual Harassment Training," which begins on page xi. For a guide and tips to using the exercises more effectively, make sure you read "How to Use This Book Most Effectively" in the Resources section.

Louise Yolton Eberhardt
December, 1994

SEXUAL HARASSMENT TRAINING

This section contains information vital to conducting successful sexual harassment workshops, including preparation for training and specific items instructors should know about and expect from management, participants, and themselves.

Sexual harassment training should include both female and male facilitators to avoid gender-bias problems. Remember that although these exercises are primarily designed to educate participants about male on female harassment, it is important to acknowledge that men can also be the victims of sexual harassment. Remind the participants of this and try to include as many crossover examples as possible.

Behavior that many women or courts would label as sexual harassment has often been accepted as normal in the workplace. Women have been expected to tolerate off-color jokes, demeaning remarks, sexual innuendos, and obscene cartoons. In some organizations they may even have to face activities as offensive as strippers performing at retirement parties. These behaviors are often the result of our gender role socialization, so training should always include examining socialization messages that no longer fit today's workplace. For all workshops, make sure to include at least one of the following exercises: #5, "It's Only Natural;" #6, "Dispelling the Myths;" #7, "Nice Women Don't;" or #8, "A Power Issue." For a guide to using the exercises effectively, make sure that you read "How to Use This Book Most Effectively" in the Resources section.

PROBLEM IDENTIFICATION

Before offering any training to an organization, find out the type and the level of sexual harassment it has experienced or is currently dealing with (very few organizations can claim they are totally free of harassment). An assessment will allow you to better plan which exercises you should choose as well as provide you with some real examples you can use during the workshop.

Gathering focus groups of target employees, such as lower level women, higher level women, lower level men, higher level men, will help you quickly and effectively gather concrete data on the organization's problems and needs as well as determine what kind of exercises will work best for that particular organization. If you develop focus groups, make sure that you separate them by gender. Some trainers like to follow up with individual interviews, questionnaires, or surveys; if you use these methods, make sure the process remains confidential.

Typical questions to ask during the assessment process include:

1. To what extent is sexual harassment a problem in this organization?

2. What specific behaviors would you include in your definition of sexual harassment?

3. Are senior level managers committed to a harassment-free workplace? How do they display their commitment or lack of commitment?

4. Does your organization have a sexual harassment policy and if so, what is it? Is it effective?

5. Do your supervisors/managers communicate any information about sexual harassment? If yes, what? If no, are they denying that an issue exists or avoiding the issue?

6. Do employees feel comfortable reporting sexual harassment or are they fearful of reprisals?

7. What is the complaint process? Is it effective?

8. What are some examples of sexual harassment you have experienced or witnessed in this organization?

9. How widespread is sexual harassment in this organization? Does it involve only a few employees or many? Is it the norm?

10. How are employees, especially men, responding to the issue of sexual harassment in this organization?

MANAGEMENT SUPPORT

Senior management support and commitment to a harassment-free workplace is critical to ensure effective training. Without their commitment and support the training will not work.

Share the results of the needs assessment with senior managers, invite some of them to be involved in reviewing the design of the training, and conduct the exercises first for them to obtain their feedback about changes needed in the design and their support of the training.

If the company has not established a sexual harassment policy, hold a management session to develop one (see exercise #17, "Creating a Policy"). Combine this working session with the results of the needs assessment. Be sure that the company has a policy and grievance procedure in place before the training starts.

The letter from a senior manager or team should go out to members of the organization announcing the upcoming sexual harassment training. It should indicate management's commitment and strong support of eliminating sexual harassment in the organization, the goals and broad outline of the training, and whether attendance is mandatory (usually it is, especially for supervisors and managers). This should then be followed up with a second letter containing specific information about particular sessions.

Management support can also be demonstrated by having them kick off each training session. This makes an excellent way for management to display its commitment and to clarify its stand on the issue.

PARTICIPANTS

Some facilitators believe that sexual harassment training should be offered first to senior level management, then to lower level managers and supervisors, and finally to all general employees. This model can be effective, but trainers will also find that workshops combining supervisors and employees encourage supervisors to get beyond any denial of organizational problems. However, *never* put subordinates and their immediate supervisors together in the same class.

Most of the exercises in this book have been designed to generate active participation. Discussing various sexual harassment topics may generate strong feelings in some participants, including resistance, hostility, confusion, hurt, pain, and denial. As a facilitator, be prepared to deal with these feelings.

In many organizations, you will encounter denial that sexual harassment problems exist. This is to be expected because, if participants haven't witnessed or experienced the negative results of sexual harassment personally, they may have difficulty perceiving the problem. They may also simply not wish to see changes in how men interact with women in their organization. During training—especially in hostile work environments—it is important that you encourage female participants (who are comfortable doing so) to share personal experiences in order to help men understand the damage caused by sexual harassment. However, be aware that women also feel pressure to deny a problem, even though they may be experiencing direct harassment themselves. Women often feel that if they openly complain they will receive retaliation, or they may want to try and fit in to get ahead. Also, because experiences with sexual harassment are very painful for many women, they often attempt to forget them in order to get on with their lives.

INSTRUCTORS

Instructors or facilitators can either be from outside or inside the organization; combining inside and outside trainers as a team creates an especially effective workshop, as each facilitator brings different skills and knowledge to the sessions. For example, an outside consultant trainer brings the overall knowledge and skills for facilitating a sexual harassment workshop while the internal facilitators bring knowledge of the organization and its specific sexual harassment and gender problems.

Sexual harassment trainers should have a good understanding of sexism, sexual harassment and the laws governing it, and of other diversity issues such as racism and heterosexism. Facilitators should also have a solid base of group process skills, including the skills to create a climate of trust so participants feel safe in exploring sexual harassment issues. They need to be alert to how participants are feeling, responding, or resisting.

The exercises in this book work most effectively when facilitators possess most of the following qualities:

1. Awareness of their own values, biases, and comfort with diversity;

2. Understanding of group learning processes;

3. Flexibility while conducting the exercise and the unanticipated situations that arise in them;

4. Knowledge about sexual harassment laws, including the most recent changes;

5. Respect for diversity and acceptance of participants' various styles—allowing all members the freedom to participate in their own way and at their own pace;

6. Ability to establish an informal, warm, and supportive atmosphere using a relaxed approach;

7. Ability to deal with highly-charged emotional issues;

8. Ability to handle participant resistance and denial;

9. Ability to remain open to the feedback of participants in order to learn about her- or himself.

Defining Problems

DEFINING PROBLEMS

1 WHY ARE WE HERE? (p 3)

Participants gather to discuss workshop goals, methods, and roles after a senior level manager sets the framework. (1 hour)

2 TEST YOUR KNOWLEDGE (p 6)

Participants test their knowledge of sexual harassment by answering a sexual harassment awareness survey and discussing their answers. ($1\frac{1}{2}$ hours)

3 WHAT IS SEXUAL HARASSMENT? (p 14)

The facilitator delivers a chalktalk to help participants better understand sexual harassment, its legal definition, and other aspects of this complex issue. (1 hour)

4 IS THIS SEXUAL HARASSMENT? (p 19)

Using actual sexual harassment cases, participants examine various scenarios to further explore and better understand what constitutes sexual harassment. (2 hours)

1 WHY ARE WE HERE?

Participants gather to discuss workshop goals, methods, and roles after a senior level manager sets the framework.

GOALS

To establish a positive learning environment.

To present an overview of the training session and develop group guidelines.

To emphasize the importance of the session and participation in it.

To demonstrate organizational support.

GROUP SIZE

Unlimited.

TIME

1 hour.

MATERIALS

Easel and easel pad; magic markers; masking tape.

PROCESS

Activity 1: Setting the Tone

1. Have a senior level manager introduce and set the tone for the session by discussing some of the following topics:
   - The organization's posture and policy regarding sexual harassment
   - A brief highlight of the sexual harassment problems in the organization, if any, and need for preventive approach
   - Management's zero tolerance of sexual harassment
   - Overall focus of the training:
     - To help everyone understand the issues of sexual harassment, the law, how to create a harassment-free environment, and who will receive training and when

2. Have the senior manager introduce and highlight the credentials of the training staff.

☞ *This is a good point for the senior manager to exit, but discuss when they would like to leave prior to the exercise. Some senior managers may like to stay to hear and respond to participants' concerns. In some organizations, however, their continued presence may inhibit participants from sharing their honest feelings.*

Activity 2: Inclusion

1. Welcome participants and make any appropriate remarks regarding their organization or department.

2. Find out how participants feel about being part of the seminar by asking each to complete the following open-ended sentences:

   ☞ *Write the questions on an easel sheet for all to see and ask for a volunteer to start the process.*

   • My name is . . . and I work at . . .

   • For me, exploring sexual harassment in this forum is . . .

   • A concern I have about the training session is . . .

   • I hope I'll come away with . . .

   • The questions I would like answered during this workshop are . . .

3. When all the participants have shared their feelings, make appropriate comments about their responses.

Activity 3: Workshop Overview

1. Present an overview of the training session, making sure to include the following:

   • The overall goals for the training

   • The training methods and process that will be used

   • Any housekeeping information, such as locations of rest rooms and break rooms, when breaks will take place, how telephone messages will be related, etc.

   • Roles of the staff

   • Workshop schedule and topic overview

2. Lead a brainstorming session in which participants develop guidelines as to how the group would like to work together (e.g., confidentiality, honesty, risk taking, active participation, no personal attacks, disagreements are OK, etc.).

    ☞ *Record the guidelines on the easel chart and refine them until all group members agree to follow them.*

©1995 Whole Person Press   210 W Michigan Duluth MN 55802   (800) 247-6789

2 TEST YOUR KNOWLEDGE

Participants test their knowledge of sexual harassment by answering a sexual harassment awareness survey and discussing their answers.

GOALS

To discover what participants already know about sexual harassment.

To begin discussing sexual harassment, especially what it is and how it operates.

To begin discussion about sexual harassment in a nondefensive manner.

GROUP SIZE

Unlimited.

TIME

$1\frac{1}{2}$ hours.

MATERIALS

Easel and easel pad; magic markers; **Sexual Harassment Awareness** worksheets; **Awareness Answers** worksheets.

☞ *Prior to the exercise, prepare an easel sheet with a continuum scale numbered 1–10.*

PROCESS

Activity 1: Ice Breaker

1. Introduce the topic with the following chalktalk:
   - Many people in the workplace are confused about what constitutes sexual harassment.
   - Some of you may resent being here to receive yet another seminar on sexual harassment.
   - Others may be wondering why this organization is spending money and energy educating you when you feel the problem doesn't exist in your workplace.
   - People view sexual harassment in very different ways.

©1995 Whole Person Press   210 W Michigan Duluth MN 55802   (800) 247-6789

- Because of this, we will start by learning how much you already know about sexual harassment.

2. Display the continuum scale and give participants the following instructions:

  ➤ Consider how much you know about sexual harassment issues and laws.

  ➤ In a moment, I will ask you to rate your sexual harassment knowledge level on a scale from 1 to 10, where 1 means you lack any knowledge and 10 means you know everything there is to know about sexual harassment.

3. Ask each participant where they think they lie on the scale and place a check under the appropriate number for each response.

4. Lead a discussion using the following questions:

  ✔ What does the scale indicate about this group's sexual harassment awareness?

  ✔ How much time have you spent in the last year reading about or discussing sexual harassment with colleagues, friends, or family members?

  ✔ What impact has your reading or discussion had on you?

Activity 2: Sexual Harassment Awareness

1. Distribute copies of the **Sexual Harassment Awareness** worksheets and allow participants 5–10 minutes to honestly answer each of the questions.

2. Review the survey question by question, leading a discussion about participants' replies.

   ☞ *Do not give them the correct answers until they have had a chance to debate with each other. See the answer sheet for information about the answers.*

3. Distribute copies of the **Awareness Answers** worksheets and allow participants time to check their replies against the answers and discuss where they were right and wrong.

4. Close by asking each participant to share how they now feel about exploring sexual harassment in a more in-depth manner.

VARIATIONS

■ Turn Activity 2 into a contest by forming small groups for discussion during *Step 2,* instructing the groups to come to a consensus on each question. Then read the correct answers from the answer worksheets and keep track of which group had the most right.

■ If you have time after Activity 2, have participants generate a list of questions they have about sexual harassment. Record these questions and make sure all of them have been answered by the end of the training session.

©1995 Whole Person Press   210 W Michigan Duluth MN 55802   (800) 247-6789

SEXUAL HARASSMENT AWARENESS

1. When I think of sexual harassment:
   - ❑ I'm not sure what it is.
   - ❑ The definition is confusing and unclear to me.
   - ❑ I'm not sure about the boundaries between sexual harassment and harmless flirting.
   - ❑ I think of it as a tool women use against men.
   - ❑ I understand the law and the behavior it defines.

2. Of the following behaviors, check those that you think are part of the definition of sexual harassment.
   - ❑ Male employees rating their female colleagues according to their physical attractiveness—including comments about their breasts and hips—as they pass an area where the men are working
   - ❑ Pinups on the office or plant walls
   - ❑ Talking about one's sexual exploits at work in a very graphic way
   - ❑ Job-related threats to gain sexual favors
   - ❑ A single request for a date
   - ❑ "Accidentally" brushing sexual parts of someone's body
   - ❑ Sexual innuendoes and dirty jokes

3. Sexual harassment can involve which of the following:
   - ❑ A man harassing a woman
   - ❑ A man harassing a man
   - ❑ A woman harassing a man
   - ❑ A woman harassing a woman

4. Women who file sexual harassment complaints:
   - ❑ Are committing career suicide
   - ❑ Are labeled as trouble makers
   - ❑ Are often lying
   - ❑ Usually wait until the behavior has gotten very serious

SEXUAL HARASSMENT AWARENESS, continued

5. Most harassers are (check one):
    - ❑ Harmless flirts
    - ❑ Looking for a sexual partner
    - ❑ Trying to intimidate and humiliate the other person
    - ❑ Violent men

6. Targets of sexual harassment take the following actions: (check all that apply)
    - ❑ Quit their job
    - ❑ Try to ignore the behavior
    - ❑ Try to avoid the harasser
    - ❑ File a formal complaint or seek legal help
    - ❑ Go along with the behavior, acting as if they enjoy it
    - ❑ Tell the harasser to stop
    - ❑ Tell others about the harassment
    - ❑ Grin and bear it to protect their careers

7. The typical harasser is (check all that apply):
    - ❑ Man who is older than the target
    - ❑ Married and of the same ethnic background of the target
    - ❑ A chronic harasser who sexually harasses one person after another
    - ❑ Sexually insecure

True or False? (circle one):

T F 8. An organization can be held responsible for a harasser's actions, even in cases in which the employer has no actual knowledge of the harassment.

T F 9. An organization is responsible for creating a harassment-free workplace. This includes monitoring the behavior of third parties such as clients and vendors or contractors.

T F 10. Women bring harassment problems on themselves by dressing or acting provocatively.

©1995 Whole Person Press   210 W Michigan Duluth MN 55802   (800) 247-6789

SEXUAL HARASSMENT AWARENESS, continued

T F 11. The intent of the person engaging in behavior others may identify as harassment is important in sexual harassment cases.

T F 12. If someone is harassed at an after-hours office party, the action is considered to have happened as part of the victim's social life and cannot be considered workplace sexual harassment.

T F 13. Most reasonable people consider positive comments about their physical body as a compliment and not as sexual harassment.

T F 14. If a person is making comments about what he likes sexually about his partner to a coworker and another person overhears it, that third party cannot claim sexual harassment.

T F 15. Harassers may be open to civil and criminal charges and may also place their organization at risk.

T F 16. Not all harassers are supervisors; coworker sexual harassment is on the rise and expected to continue its increase.

T F 17. People harass others because they are attracted to them.

T F 18. Women in jobs traditionally held by men are more likely to be victims of harassment than are other women.

©1995 Whole Person Press   210 W Michigan Duluth MN 55802   (800) 247-6789

AWARENESS ANSWERS

1. This question is to help people think about their knowledge of sexual harassment. The only false response is: "I think of it as a tool women use against men." In reality, it is behavior perpetrators use against their victims to intimidate and humiliate them.

2. The only answer that is not part of the definition of sexual harassment is "a single request for a date." All the others could be sexual harassment and are usually unwelcome by women.

3. All the answers are correct, although most harassment occurs with men harassing women.

4. The only answer that is not correct is "are often lying." Victims have more to lose than to gain by filing a complaint. Only 3–7% of harassment victims ever file complaints.

5. The correct answer is "trying to intimidate and humiliate the other person." Sexual harassment is about power, not sex (although some men who think they are only flirting or looking for a sexual partner may be engaging in sexual harassment and not know it).

6. All the responses can be correct, but few women ever file complaints, tell the harasser to stop, or even tell others about what happened. Most try to ignore it (65%) or try to avoid the harasser (48%), and most just grin and bear it to protect their career. (1981 Merit System Protection Board Study.)

7. All the answers apply.

8. **True**. Supervisors are considered by law to be agents of the organization and to have a responsibility to know what is going on in their organization.

9. **True**. When an organization is told about harassing behavior they are expected to take immediate and appropriate corrective action in situations that can be controlled.

AWARENESS ANSWERS, continued

10. **False**. Both men and women often agree with this statement and blame the victim. There is, however, no evidence that women who dress or act conservatively are not sexually harassed. In fact they are.

11. **False**. It is the impact of the behavior that counts, not the intent. The focus is on how the recipient perceives and reacts to the behavior.

12. **False**. An office function is still considered the workplace. If coworkers, however, were at a social function like a public base-ball game, then harassment would not be the responsibility of the organization, unless a supervisor or manager engaged in the behavior.

13. **False**. Most reasonable women would not consider comments in the workplace about their bodies to be compliments at work. Men perceive it differently, thinking of the remarks as compliments. A 1991 *Newsweek* poll showed that almost 70% of the men but less than 20% of the women said they considered receiving a sexual proposition to be flattering.

14. **False**. If the conversation is helping to create a hostile work environment or is interfering with the person's work performance, it can be considered sexual harassment.

15. **True**. Both the organization and the harasser have been found liable by the courts and have had to pay damages for sexual harassment.

16. **True**. Men, in particular, use gender power to sexually harass women colleagues.

17. **False**. People who harass others want to intimidate them.

18. **True**. According to a Merit Systems study, women in jobs tradi-tionally held by men are 25% more likely to be targets of harass-ment than are other women. This may be because some men feel threatened by competing with women in jobs they consider their "turf" and feel insecure if a woman should surpass them or do better at a job they believe only men are supposed to do.

3 WHAT IS SEXUAL HARASSMENT?

The facilitator delivers a chalktalk to help participants better understand sexual harassment, its legal definition, and other aspects of this complex issue.

GOALS

To define sexual harassment.

To help participants understand what sexual harassment is and how it operates in the workplace.

To help participants gain an understanding of sexual harassment's legal implications.

GROUP SIZE

Unlimited.

TIME

1 hour.

MATERIALS

Easel and easel pad; magic markers; **Sexual Harassment Definitions** worksheets.

PROCESS

Activity 1: Definitions

1. Lead a brainstorming session to create a list of words that describe sexual harassment.

    ☞ *Note that usually no one will use the word "illegal" and use this observation to segue to the next step.*

2. Use the following chalktalk to highlight the elements of sexual harassment:

    • Sexual harassment is any unwelcome words or actions of a sexual nature that create an intimidating, hostile, or offensive working environment.

- Most instances involve a man sexually harassing a woman.
- However, sexual harassment can also be:
  - A woman harassing a man
  - A woman harassing a woman
  - A man harassing a man
- Sexual harassment can come from anyone: a supervisor, a professor, a coworker, a client, a vendor, or a contractor.
- In simple terms, sexual harassment is any offensive conduct related to a person's gender that a reasonable person should not have to endure—it defines a person as a sex object rather than a professional.
- Sexual harassment is about power and intimidation and carries a hidden or not-so-hidden threat to the victim's job.

3. Present the Equal Employment Opportunity Commission's definition of sexual harassment:

- In general, the Equal Employment Opportunity Commission guidelines say that any unwelcome sexual advances, requests for sexual favors, and other verbal or physical conduct of a sexual nature is sexual harassment when:
  - It is made a term or condition of employment or academic advancement—your job depends on your response.

    ☞ *Ask for and add any examples that help explain, such as a supervisor implying that keeping one's job depends on sharing a room on a business trip.*

  - It is used as the basis for employment or academic decisions, such as raises, promotions, assignments, grades, etc.

    ☞ *Ask for and offer examples to help explain, such as a supervisor transferring an employee who refuses a request for a date.*

  - It creates an offensive or hostile working or academic environment or negatively interferes with a person's work or academic performance.

4. Explain to participants that the last condition of the Equal Employment Opportunity Commission's definition is often confusing (offensive or hostile working environment), and that two facilitators will perform a role play to help illustrate it more clearly.

    ☞ *Prepare the role play with a male and female facilitator prior to the exercise. Have the woman harass the man in ways that verbally and/or physically illustrate the last condition and have the man accept the harassment without confronting the harasser. The role play might include sexual innuendos, misogynist humor, lewd remarks, and physical touching. It is helpful if they reflect typical situations that would occur in the participants' organization.*

5. Have the facilitators act out the role play.

6. Discuss the role play with the participants, explaining that this form of harassment—creation of a hostile work environment—is difficult to define because male harassers often do not perceive their behavior as wrong but rather as normal male behavior.

7. Review all the forms sexual harassment can take by reading the items included on the worksheet.

   ☞ *It is helpful to have the key items written on a easel sheet. Unless you want participants to write additional notes, do not distribute copies of the worksheet until you have finished discussing the various forms.*

8. Distribute copies of the worksheet and ask participants if they have any questions about the definition of sexual harassment.

9. Conclude by emphasizing the following points:

   • Sexual harassment depends on how the person being harassed is affected and not on the harasser's intent; giving in does not necessarily mean that the conduct was welcome.

   • Laws do not restrict normal socializing between women and men; people can still give each other compliments or ask someone out on a date—but remember: "no" means "no."

   • An excellent guideline is to keep feedback related to business.

VARIATIONS

■ Show a video that provides examples of sexual harassment in organizations. There are many available today from various video companies.

■ If you do not feel comfortable discussing legal issues, invite a civil rights or human resource expert to speak and answer questions about the law and company policy and procedures.

SEXUAL HARASSMENT DEFINITIONS

The Equal Employment Opportunity Commission's
Definition of Sexual Harassment

Harassment on the basis of sex is a violation of [the law].

Unwelcome sexual advances, requests for sexual favors and other verbal or physical conduct of a sexual nature constitute sexual harassment when:

1. submission to such conduct is made either explicitly or implicitly a term or condition of an individual's employment,

2. submission to or rejection of such conduct by an individual is used as the basis for employment decisions affecting such individual, or

3. such conduct has the purpose or effect of unreasonably interfering with an individual's work performance or creating an intimidating, hostile or offensive working environment.

Forms of Sexual Harassment:

1. Verbal Examples:

    - Sexual jokes or teasing, misogynist humor

    - Innuendos and off-color remarks

    - Comments about how someone looks, especially about parts of the body

    - Catcalls, whistles and forms of address: honey, babe, etc.

    - Pressure for dates

2. Visual Examples:

    - Presence of sexual visual material, such as pinups, cartoons, graffiti, computer programs, catalogs of a sexual nature

    - Written material that is sexual in nature, such as notes or E-mail containing sexual comments

    - Staring or leering

    - Suggestive gestures or looks, smacking of lips, hand gestures, or elevator eyes

SEXUAL HARASSMENT DEFINITIONS, continued

3. Physical Contact:

    • Unwelcome hugging, sexual touching, or kissing

    • Pinching, grabbing or patting

    • Standing too close to or brushing against another person

    • Cornering, trapping, or blocking a person's pathway

    • Excessively "lengthy" sexual handshakes

    • Rape or attempted rape

    • Sexual assault or forced fondling

4 IS THIS SEXUAL HARASSMENT?

Using actual sexual harassment cases, participants examine various scenarios to further explore and better understand what constitutes sexual harassment.

GOALS

To increase participants' knowledge of sexual harassment.

To gain a better understanding of the legal issues involved in sexual harassment.

GROUP SIZE

Up to 35 participants.

TIME

2 hours.

MATERIALS

Easel and easel pad; magic markers; masking tape; **Sexual Harassment Case Scenario's (A–I)** worksheets; **Court Rulings (A–I)** worksheets.

PROCESS

☞ *This exercise is best conducted after the legal definitions found in Exercise #3, "What Is Sexual Harassment?" have been presented.*

1. Begin the exercise with the following chalktalk:
   - Most sexual harassment incidents involve the same basic legal issues.
   - Courts use these four factors to determine if a person has been sexually harassed:
     - ○ Was the conduct sexual in nature?
     - ○ Was the conduct unreasonable?
     - ○ Was the conduct severe or pervasive in the workplace?
     - ○ Was the conduct unwelcome?
   - The focus of this session is to give you a working knowledge of sexual harassment as it is defined by law and interpreted by the Equal Employment Opportunity Commission and the courts.

☞ *If you have not conducted Exercise #3, "What Is Sexual Harassment?" present the definitions of sexual harassment as explained in that exercise before proceeding.*

2. Form no more than 7 groups of 5 participants and give them the following assignment:

   ➤ In a minute I will distribute an actual case scenario to each group.

   ➤ Read the scenario, discuss it, and decide whether it constitutes sexual harassment based on your understanding and interpretation of the law.

   ➤ Use the 4 legal questions presented a few minutes ago as a guideline.

     ☞ *Write the questions on an easel sheet so participants can refer to them.*

   ➤ Describe why your group decided the scenario did or did not constitute sexual harassment and record your conclusions on an easel sheet.

   ➤ You will have 15 minutes for this task, after which you will report your decision to the entire group.

3. Distribute a different scenario issue to each group and allow them 15 minutes to complete the task.

   ☞ *If you have fewer than 7 groups, distribute the remaining scenarios equally and allow more time as needed. As participants work on the task, move from group to group and help clarify their task. Do not, however, give them the correct answers.*

4. Reconvene the entire group and have each small group report their results using the following process:

   a. Have a representative from the group with Scenario A read their worksheet so everyone understands the situation.

     ☞ *You may want to distribute the worksheet for that scenario to all participants at this time.*

   b. Have another participant from the same group display his or her group's easel sheet and explain how they arrived at their conclusion. Other participants from that group should feel free to add points of clarification whenever necessary.

   c. Allow participants from the observing groups to ask the presenting group questions about their conclusion.

   d. Read the actual court ruling from the **Court Rulings** worksheet and lead a brief discussion about the ruling and the group's conclusion.

©1995 Whole Person Press   210 W Michigan Duluth MN 55802   (800) 247-6789

5. Repeat the process until each group has reported its conclusions and thank all the participants for their hard work.

VARIATION

■ If you are short on time, do not form small groups. Simply read the cases and lead a brief discussion in the entire group before sharing the court rulings.

SEXUAL HARASSMENT
CASE SCENARIO A

A female welder works in a shipyard with many male employees. Of the almost 850 skilled craft workers employed there, only 6 are women. Displayed on the walls are various pictures (at least 30) which she is uncomfortable seeing when she has to walk through or work in these areas. The pictures include a nude woman wearing high heels and holding a whip, tool company posters depicting nude women bending over with their buttocks and genitals exposed, a picture of a woman's pubic area and a meat spatula, a dart board with a drawing of a woman's breast and nipple as the bull's eye, and another picture showing a frontal view of a female torso with the words "U.S.D.A. Choice" written on it. There are no similar pictures of men displayed. The woman complains repeatedly to her supervisors about the pictures, but they do nothing. One of the supervisors tells her that the company has no policy against such pictures and the men have a constitutional right to post them. There are no women in any supervisory positions.

Does this woman have a case for sexual harassment?

If no, explain why not.

If yes, explain why.

SEXUAL HARASSMENT
CASE SCENARIOS B & C

Case History B

A woman attorney who works in a federal agency says that her agency is run like a brothel. Senior attorneys have affairs with secretaries and junior attorneys. The women who participate in the affairs are given preferential treatment in the form of cash bonuses and promotions. When she complains to management, she receives poor reviews and is threatened with dismissal.

Case History C

A male supervisor propositions several of the female employees during daily walks around the office. Later he is heard to say that he is promoting one woman because "she knows how to make me feel good."

Are these cases of sexual harassment?

If no, why not.

If yes, explain why.

SEXUAL HARASSMENT
CASE SCENARIOS D & E

Case History D

A woman employee walks toward the door of the office building and finds a male supervisor blocking the doorway; he then very forcefully twists the woman's arm.

Case History E

In a bakery plant one of the supervisors states that he doesn't think a woman should be foreman and boasts that he would make it "rough enough for her to leave." He then goes on a campaign of ridiculing a woman foreman, yelling at her, and giving her impossible tasks to do.

Do either of the women in D or E have a case for sexual harassment?

If no, explain why not.

If yes, explain why.

SEXUAL HARASSMENT
CASE SCENARIO F

A female bank employee is invited out to dinner by her supervisor. She is a former bank teller who has worked her way up to a position as assistant bank manager. She has resisted his sexual advances up to now. At dinner he suggests going to a local motel. She puts him off during the meal, but finally out of fear of losing her job, she gives in. Over the next several years he often makes demands for sexual favors during and after work. She estimates that she has had sex with him 40 or 50 times and that he raped her on more than one occasion. Also he fondled her in front of other employees, followed her into the rest room, and exposed himself to her at work. Finally she could not take it anymore, went on leave, and was fired.

Does this woman have a case for sexual harassment?

If no, explain why not.

If yes, explain why.

SEXUAL HARASSMENT
CASE SCENARIO G

A woman is hired as "Pet of the Month" by *Penthouse* magazine. Her job involves being in movies and making personal appearances in highly sexualized settings. The publisher pressures her into having sex with business associates the publisher wants to please.

Does this woman have a case for sexual harassment?

If no, explain why not.

If yes, explain why.

©1995 Whole Person Press   210 W Michigan Duluth MN 55802   (800) 247-6789

SEXUAL HARASSMENT
CASE SCENARIO H

A female agent of a government agency went out to lunch one day with a male colleague. He asked her out again for lunch and she refused. Then he started sending her love letters. One letter said, "I cried over you last night and I'm totally drained today." Another said, "I know that you are worth knowing with or without sex." She found these letters bizarre and frightening. He kept making advances and sending these letters. He once tracked her down when she was on a business trip and sent flowers and a note to her hotel room. She filed a complaint and the employer temporarily transferred the man to a different location. After three months he was brought back to her location with instructions to leave her alone.

Does this woman have a case for sexual harassment?

If no, explain why not.

If yes, explain why.

SEXUAL HARASSMENT
CASE SCENARIO I

Three female employees of a construction firm said the male employees repeatedly engaged in sexual harassment. These men made
repeated requests for sexual favors and physical touching, exposed
their genitals and buttocks, urinated in the women's water bottles and
trucks' gas tanks, refused to perform repairs on the women's trucks
unless a male user also complained, and refused the women rest
room breaks in a town near the construction site.

Do these women have a sexual harassment case?

If no, explain why not.

If yes, explain why.

SEXUAL HARASSMENT CASE SCENARIOS
COURT RULINGS – A, B, & C

Case A—Robinson v. Jacksonville Shipyards, Inc., 760 F. Supp. 1486 (M.D. Fla. 1991)

The court ruled that nude pinups in the workplace can constitute sexual harassment. In this particular case the woman won and the court ruled that posting pictures of nude and partly-nude women is a form of sexual harassment: "Pornography on an employer's wall or desk communicates a message about the way [the employer] views women, a view strikingly at odds with the way women wish to be viewed in the workplace." The judge also noted that the shipyard maintained a "boys' club" atmosphere with a constant "visual assault on the sensibilities of female workers," and that the sexualized atmosphere of the workplace had the effect of keeping women out of the shipyard. "A preexisting atmosphere that deters women from entering or continuing in a profession or job is no less destructive to and offensive to workplace equality than a sign declaring 'Men Only.'"

Case B—Broderick v. Ruder, 685 F. Supp. 1269 (D.D.C. 1988)

Case C—Toscano v. Nimmo, 570 F. Supp. 1197 (D. Del. 1983)

Both of these cases are about an employer giving preferential treatment to a person who goes along with a sexual advance. In this type of harassment, only those employees who submit to sexual demands of the supervisor are rewarded. In these situations it is the other employees who can claim sexual harassment if they are denied raises or promotions because of the sexual attention the supervisor is giving to the one going along with him or her.

In case B the court found that the federal agency, U.S. Securities and Exchange Commission, had created a hostile environment for women who complained about male supervisors giving preferential treatment to the women with whom they were having affairs. In this case it was the retaliation against those who complained that was more the sexual harassment than the actual preferential treatment.

In case C the court ruled that the supervisor's preferential treatment of his new woman friend was part of an overall pattern of discriminatory treatment toward women employees.

SEXUAL HARASSMENT CASE SCENARIOS
COURT RULINGS – D, E, & F

Case D—McKinney v. Dole, 765 F.2d 1129 (D.C. Cir. 1985)

Case E—Bell v. Crackin Good Bakers, Inc., 777 F.2d 1497 (11th Cir. 1985)

These cases are about hostile acts related to a person's gender and do not involve sexual overtures. The hostility often comes from men's opposition to women in jobs that traditionally were all male. The courts have found that sexual harassment can exist without sexual misconduct.

In Case D the court ruled in the woman's favor saying that her supervisor would not have treated a male employee in that way.

In Case E the hostile conduct is an effort to force the woman to leave her job and the workplace. The court held that "threatening, bellicose, demeaning, hostile or offensive conduct by a supervisor in the workplace because of the sex of the victim" was enough to support a claim of sexual harassment. Some people consider this a clear case of sexual discrimination, not harassment. It really isn't important what they call it because both are subject to the same legal prohibitions. The laws against sexual harassment have mostly derived from the sexual discrimination laws.

Case F—Meritor Sav. Bank v. Vinson, 477 U.S. 57 (1986)

The lower court found this was not sexual harassment because they said the relationship was voluntary and the employer wasn't liable because the woman had not complained. This ruling was appealed and the ruling was reversed. The court said her participation could not be fairly called "voluntary" because she was afraid she would lose her job if she did not go along and regardless of whether she complained the bank was liable because the supervisor is an agent of the employer. The U.S. Supreme Court affirmed this ruling and said the question was not whether she had made a voluntary decision to have sex but whether it was welcomed or not. The court said the behavior was definitely sexual harassment.

SEXUAL HARASSMENT CASE SCENARIOS
COURT RULINGS – G & H

Case G—Thoreson v. Penthouse Int'l, Ltd, 563 N.Y.S. 2d 968 (N.Y. Sup. Ct.1990)

The court found that even when a woman is hired to do a highly sexualized job, she does not waive her right to object to other forms of sexual conduct. The magazine and its publisher were held liable: "The offensiveness of defendants' conduct is not mitigated by the fact that plaintiff's job as a model and actress for Penthouse involved, in part, the commercial exploitation of her physical appearance. Sexual slavery was not a part of her job description . . . Protections against sexual harassment are arguably more necessary in a workplace permeated by conceptions of women as sex objects. When there is a significant potential for discriminatory abuse of power by an employer, the need for an effective deterrent to enforce public policy and protect employees is even greater."

Case H—Ellison v. Brady, 924 F.2d 872 (9th Cir. 1991)

The district court dismissed the case, applying the "reasonable person" test to the circumstances and ruling that the man's actions were "isolated and genuinely trivial," in effect saying that the average adult, regardless of gender, would not have found the workplace hostile. However the U.S. Court of Appeals disagreed, reversed that decision, and threw out the "reasonable person" rule. The court ruled that the hostile work environment must be judged from the viewpoint of the target, in this case the woman employee or "reasonable woman." Supervisors, especially men, may no longer disregard a complaint because they do not think the behavior is offensive. Instead they must consider the impact of the behavior on the target. The court wrote:

"Conduct that many men consider unobjectionable may offend many women. Because women are disproportionately victims of rape and sexual assault, women have a stronger incentive to be concerned with sexual behavior. Women who are victims of mild forms of sexual harassment may understandably worry whether a harasser's conduct is merely a prelude to a violent sexual assault. Men, who are rarely victims of sexual assault, may view sexual conduct in a vacuum without a full appreciation of the social setting or the underlying threat of violence that a woman may perceive."

SEXUAL HARASSMENT CASE SCENARIO
COURT RULING – I

Case I—Hall v. Gus Construction Co., 842 F.2d 1010 (8th Cir. 1988)

The firm was found guilty of sexual harassment. The court concluded that the "incidents of harassment and unequal treatment . . . would not have occurred but for the fact that [the employees] were women. Intimidation and hostility toward women because they are women can obviously result from conduct other than explicit sexual advances."

Exploring Causes

EXPLORING CAUSES

5 IT'S ONLY NATURAL

By identifying gender role socialization messages they learned as children, participants explore the connection between those ideas and sexual harassment.

GOALS

To identify the socialization messages men receive and their relationship to how they see and treat women.

To identify the socialization messages women receive and their relationship to how they see and respond to men.

To identify the connection between socialization messages and gender role behavior surrounding sexual harassment.

GROUP SIZE

Up to 25 (requires male and female participants).

TIME

1 1/2–2 hours.

MATERIALS

Easel and easel pad; magic markers; masking tape; **Gender Role Messages** worksheets.

PROCESS

Activity 1: Introduction to Gender Role Messages

Introduce the exercise's topic and goals with the following chalktalk:

- One of the major reasons sexual harassment continues to occur is due in part to the gender roles we have learned through socialization.
- The socialization of both men and women has resulted in unequal power relationships between men and women.
- Sexual harassment in the workplace is an extension of these outdated gender roles, which are inappropriate and haven't caught up with our society's rapid changes.

- The socialization messages men receive often lead them to engage in sexually-harassing behavior or to act inappropriately around women. Since this behavior is learned in childhood, it is often seen as a normal way for males to behave.

- The socialization messages women receive often affect how they respond when men sexually harass them or behave in a manner that makes them uncomfortable.

- Today we want to examine those messages and how they impact our behavior around the issues of sexual harassment.

- We will first work in separate gender groups to identify the socialization messages we received as children.

Activity 2: Gender Role Messages

1. Divide participants into same-gender groups and provide the following instructions:

    ➤ Brainstorm ideas and develop a list of the gender socialization messages you received (or still receive) that you think are connected to sexual harassment.

    ☞ *If participants seem confused about their task, provide some examples such as: "Even though most women work outside of the home, society still sends messages that men are supposed to act as breadwinners and women as homemakers. Because many people still believe that women choose to go to the workplace, they also may believe women deserve whatever treatment they receive." See the* **Gender Role Messages** *worksheets for other examples.*

2. Move the groups to separate meeting spaces and allow them 30 minutes to complete the task.

    ☞ *Have facilitators record the messages on an easel sheet as they are identified. As each group works, facilitators should add any critical messages that participants miss. See the* **Gender Role Messages** *worksheets for other examples.*

3. Reconvene the entire group and, beginning with the men, ask each gender group to read its messages.

4. Distribute copies of both **Gender Role Messages** worksheets and briefly discuss those messages that participants did not identify in their groups.

©1995 Whole Person Press   210 W Michigan Duluth MN 55802   (800) 247-6789

5. Lead a discussion about the impact of these messages on male and female behavior using the following questions:

☞ *Make sure to identify that these messages serve to enforce male dominance and female submission.*

✔ Based on these messages, how have women learned to respond to sexual harassment?

✔ Based on these messages, how have men learned to respond to sexual harassment?

☞ *Make sure participants get the point that these messages contribute to men believing that, contrary to data, sexual harassment does not occur or that the incidents are not significant or damaging.*

✔ What would be some healthier and more realistic messages to give ourselves and our children?

✔ Which of these messages have you seen reinforced in your organization?

☞ *You might point out that a double standard exists in most organizations: men and women exhibiting the same behavior are often evaluated differently. Sexual behavior in the workplace is also viewed differently by men and women.*

✔ How could you help to change these messages in your organization?

6. Form same-gender groups of 4 participants and ask them to identify and discuss the messages that need attention in order to change their attitudes as well as gender role behavior they need to alter in themselves.

GENDER ROLE MESSAGES

Messages men receive that lead to sexual harassment

- Women are only kidding when they say "no."

- Men can't be expected to ignore a good looking woman (they can't help it).

- Anybody but my sister, wife, mother.

- Women are sex objects (they don't see women as human).

- Men should have many sexual conquests.

- Only promiscuous women get harassed. Some women look like they are just asking for it.

- Boys will be boys.

- Women are not serious about their work. In fact a real woman wants to stay at home.

- A woman could discourage unwanted sexual attention if she really wanted it to stop.

- Fast women are sluts; fast men are normal or studs.

- Men should be in control and in power.

- Women use sexual harassment to get back at men.

- Women really like sexual attention at work and in public.

- If a woman is friendly to and flirtatious with a man, she wants to have sex with him.

- Women are inferior to men (so men shouldn't have to compete with them).

- Men are sexual animals.

- Men are supposed to initiate sex and relationships.

- Successful women have slept their way to the top.

- Men should be the breadwinners.

- A man's career is his life; a woman's career is just a job (so a threat to a man's career is a threat to his existence).

- If a woman raises her voice or swears in reaction to harassment, then she wasn't a lady in the first place and deserves what she gets.

GENDER ROLE MESSAGES, continued

Messages women receive that
cause them to accept sexual harassment

- The male ego is delicate; don't hurt a man's fragile ego; protect men.

- A woman is to blame if raped or sexually harassed (she did something to make him do that).

- Women should take care of and please men (and not say anything if sexually harassed).

- Nice women don't talk about sex (and don't say anything if they encounter sexual harassment; it's too embarrassing).

- A woman's self worth is determined or dependent on male attention or approval, especially when measured in terms of sexual attractiveness.

- If a woman takes a "man's job," she has to pay extra dues.

- Women should be passive, vulnerable, powerless, and act hysterical and out of control when angry.

- Angry women are bitches.

- A real lady would diffuse a sexual harassment situation by being polite and not raising her voice.

- Successful women have slept their way to the top.

- Women are to compete with other women for male attention.

- Men can't control their sexual urges.

- Women are supposed to be weak—recipients of a chivalry designed to keep them subservient to men.

©1995 Whole Person Press   210 W Michigan Duluth MN 55802   (800) 247-6789

6 DISPELLING THE MYTHS

After sharing their beliefs about sexual harassment, participants examine which beliefs are true and which are really myths.

GOALS

To discover the beliefs participants hold about sexual harassment.

To examine the impact of these beliefs on behavior.

To dispel the myths connected with sexual harassment.

GROUP SIZE

Up to 25 participants.

TIME

$1\frac{1}{2}$ hours.

MATERIALS

Easel and easel pad; magic markers; masking tape; **Sexual Harassment Beliefs** worksheets.

PROCESS

☞ *Prior to the exercise, prepare and hang belief sheets on the walls. Each sheet should include one of the statements from the Sexual Harassment Beliefs worksheets, but not the truth behind the myth [bracketed information]. Make two columns below each statement, one labelled "Men" and the other "Women."*

1. Introduce the exercise with the following chalktalk:

   • In this session you will have an opportunity to explore gender beliefs about sexual harassment as well as your own personal thoughts.

   • We are going to start with an exercise that you should find thought provoking.

   • As we conduct the exercise, keep in mind that you will get the most out of it if you are open and honest.

2. Present the following instructions for the exercise:

   ➤ The sheets hanging around the room contain various beliefs about men and women, especially issues that relate to sexual harassment.

©1995 Whole Person Press   210 W Michigan Duluth MN 55802   (800) 247-6789

➤ Take a magic marker, go to each sheet, and make a check mark under your gender only if you believe the statement.

➤ Make an "X" under your gender only if you do not believe the statement but feel your gender in general believes it.

➤ Do not talk while you are doing this—we will have an opportunity to discuss each statement later.

➤ After you have gone to each sheet, take a brief break until I call everyone back. Do not wander far away.

3. Distribute the magic markers and tell them to start.

4. When all have finished, reconvene the group and present the following chalktalk:

- Women and men often see the same behavior very differently.

- Attitudes about behavior stem from the socialization messages we received growing up and, in some cases, still receive today.

- Part of what we learned is misinformation about gender attitudes and behavior.

- We will now examine the work we just did and explore which of the beliefs are actually myths many women and men believe are true.

5. Form groups of 5 participants, give each group a roughly-equal number of belief sheets from the wall, and provide the following instructions:

➤ Decide whether each statement is a fact or a myth.

➤ If you think the belief is really a myth, record what you think the real fact is on the sheet.

➤ Count the check marks and Xs and discuss what they indicate and imply for the workplace.

➤ Take about 20 minutes for the discussion and be prepared to report the results of your work.

☞ *Move from group to group to see how each is proceeding and help those that need it.*

6. After all have finished, reconvene the entire group and have each group report their work using the following process:

a. Select one group to begin and have them share the results of their discussion of their first belief sheet.

b. Ask the rest of the group whether they agree that the statement is a myth or is true.

c. Share the truth behind the myth by reading the corresponding bracketed information from the **Sexual Harassment Beliefs** worksheets.

d. Have the entire group briefly discuss the impact of this belief on the behavior of women and men in the workplace and how they could change the myth and replace it with more realistic information.

e. Move on to the group's next sheet and repeat the process until each group has reported their work on all of their worksheets.

7. Conclude by distributing copies of the **Sexual Harassment Beliefs** worksheets and encouraging participants to counteract these myths whenever they encounter them in the workplace.

VARIATIONS

■ Develop your own belief sheets tailored to specific groups.

■ If you conducted Exercise #5, "It's Only Natural," use the lists of messages developed in Activity 2. Eliminate *Step 2* and have each gender group go through the message sheets, discussing whether each message is a myth and identifying the truth behind it. Then reconvene the group to share their list of myths.

SEXUAL HARASSMENT BELIEFS

- **If a woman is friendly and smiles at a man it is an indication that she wants to have sex with him.**

  [Myth. In a recent study, males thought females were more sexually attracted to them than the women reported. Women have been socialized to smile even when angry.]

- **Women are "asking for it" when they wear provocative clothing.**

  [Myth. Organizations should have professional dress codes appropriate to the job. However, a woman's appearance usually has more to do with her interpretation of fashion than seduction on the job, and it does not give license to break the law. Some organizations also require women to dress in a sexually provocative way (waitresses, etc.)]

- **Women appreciate comments about their appearance at work and view them as compliments.**

  [Myth. Most women want comments at work to be about their work, not about how they look. Many of the comments women get are not "You look nice today," but "You should wear that outfit more often, it shows off your great figure." Even a so-called mundane comment is often accompanied by "elevator eyes" or leers with sexual overtones. It may be true that many women do not mind the occasional nonsexual comment about their appearance, but if that is the only feedback they receive, they may feel that they are perceived as sex objects.]

- **Most charges of sexual harassment are false; women lie about sexual harassment to get back at men.**

  [Myth. False reports are rare and most sexually-harassed women do not report it or tell anyone about it. In reality, women have little to gain from filing sexual harassment charges and a lot to lose.]

- **A woman who takes a man's job deserves whatever treatment she gets.**

  [Myth. There is no longer male entitlement to certain jobs. Men must get used to competing with women professionally and not use power or intimidation to punish women who work in what used to be considered male jobs.]

SEXUAL HARASSMENT BELIEFS, continued

- **A woman could discourage unwanted sexual attention if she really wanted it to stop.**

  [Myth. This belief is a way for men to rationalize their behavior. At times people can stop sexual harassment by saying it is unwelcome and telling the perpetrator to stop. However, in some situations the behavior continues no matter what the woman does. And women fear their careers will be in jeopardy if they speak up.]

- **Sexual harassment is simply a crude form of socializing common only to certain segments of the population.**

  [Myth. Sexual harassment is found in all types of work settings and is committed by doctors, professors, and managers as well as those with blue collar jobs, such as construction workers, fire fighters, etc.]

- **Incompetent workers who fear losing their jobs file sexual harassment claims to protect themselves.**

  [Myth. Often women keep quiet when in training or on probation at work, but when they fail the training they feel they have nothing to lose by reporting the harassment they received. The harassment can also impact work performance, which is perhaps the perpetrator's intent— to get the woman out of the workplace.]

- **Sexual harassment must not have happened because the so-called victim didn't complain at the time.**

  [Myth. Most women do not talk about the problem to anyone; they instead try to block it out or grin and bear it.]

- **A certain amount of male control or domination and sexism is normal and acceptable.**

  [Myth. While this behavior is common, it is not acceptable. Until women and men stop believing this, the workplace will not change.]

- **Sexual harassment affects only a few women.**

  [Myth. Studies reporting various figures demonstrate that more than half the women who work outside the home say they have been sexually harassed in the workplace at some time during their career.]

©1995 Whole Person Press   210 W Michigan Duluth MN 55802   (800) 247-6789

SEXUAL HARASSMENT BELIEFS, continued

- **Men can't control urges or behavior—"boys will be boys."**

  [Myth. Most men usually are able to control their behavior around their mothers, in church, etc. Men need to take responsibility for their own behavior and quit blaming women. Besides, sexual harassment has more to do with power than sex .]

- **If a person ignores sexual harassment, it will go away.**

  [Myth. In reality the harassment often persists and intensifies. Ignoring it may be seen as assent or encouragement.]

- **Successful women have "slept their way to the top."**

  [Myth. Although it could happen with either men or women, this behavior most often leads to women being fired or gossiped about, not promoted. This statement is sometimes made to insult someone and avoid acknowledging hard work and skills.]

- **Women should take care of men and protect their fragile egos.**

  [Myth. Everyone is responsible for their own self esteem. However, many women believe this and feel women should not complain about sexual harassment, which would hurt the man or his career.]

- **Sexual harassment happens only to promiscuous women.**

  [Myth. Women of all personality types, not just those of a promiscuous nature, can be victims of harassment.]

- **Nice women don't get harassed.**

  [Myth. Again, women of all personality types, including "nice," can be victims of harassment. This belief also reinforces the myth that only promiscuous and willing women are harassed.]

- **Only uptight and maladjusted women with sexual and social hang-ups claim to have been harassed.**

  [Myth. Once again, all types of women are harassed.]

- **"No" means "yes."**

  [Myth. Both women and men believe this message. People must take "no" as "no" in the workplace. Women need to say no emphatically and directly; often they soften a "no" to avoid hurting a man's feelings.]

©1995 Whole Person Press   210 W Michigan Duluth MN 55802   (800) 247-6789

7 NICE WOMEN DON'T

By approaching the issue from different sides, male and female participants gain an understanding of how women typically respond to sexual harassment.

GOALS

To identify sexual harassment victims' fears about speaking up.

To understand that, simply because employees do not complain about sexual harassment does not mean that it doesn't exist.

To develop an understanding of how women typically respond to sexual harassment.

GROUP SIZE

Unlimited.

TIME

1 hour.

MATERIALS

Easel and easel pad; magic markers; masking tape.

PROCESS

Activity 1: Fears About Speaking Up

1. Introduce the exercise with the following chalktalk:

   - Most victims of workplace sexual harassment do not speak up about the incidents.

   - Even fewer ever use their company's complaint system.

   - The few who do speak up often wait until the harassment has become severe.

   - For example, most women have been socialized to avoid making trouble—they worry about being labeled by others if they speak up.

   - Today we will explore the reasons why victims stay silent and how they typically handle sexual harassment when it occurs.

☞ *If you have already conducted Exercise #5 or #6, provide additional examples based on participants' work in either of those exercises.*

2. Divide participants into same-gender groups and provide the following instructions:

➤ The women are to identify their fears about speaking up when sexually harassed—your reasons for not saying anything.

➤ The men are to identify the typical reaction of other people when they hear a woman complain she has been sexually harassed.

➤ Record this information on an easel sheet and be prepared to report your work.

3. Move the groups to separate rooms and allow them 20 minutes to complete their tasks.

4. Reconvene the entire group and, beginning with the men, have each group report their results.

☞ *It is important to point out that men often have a very different perceptions of sexual harassment. For example, one study (Gutek, University of Arizona) found that 67 percent of men would feel complimented if propositioned by a woman at work, as opposed to 17 percent of women; 63 percent of women and 15 percent of men would be insulted.* Harvard Business Review *found a similar difference: 15 percent of women and 75 percent of men said they would be flattered by sexual advances at work. Some men don't recognize that behavior such as flirting, sexual teasing, sexual remarks and innuendo—is sexual harassment. Some also want to blame the victim, the way she dressed, or how she behaved: "What did she expect, socializing in the bar after work with the men?" or "She is just a trouble maker or poor performer." They may also try to invalidate or discount the victim's feelings: "I was just kidding; can't she take a joke?" or "I was only giving her a compliment." And men who do stand up for the target are often seen by other men as "breaking rank."*

5. After both groups have reported their results, add any points they did not cover, such as:

• Fear of retaliation:

○ Women don't want to be labeled as trouble makers or people who are too sensitive, can't take it, or have no sense of humor.

©1995 Whole Person Press   210 W Michigan Duluth MN 55802   (800) 247-6789

    ○ Men often come to the man's defense and freeze out the woman.

    ○ If a woman does complain, she is often subjected to scrutiny, criticism, hostility, and blame.

- Women often fear no one will believe them. If they have waited until the harassment becomes severe before speaking out, they will be questioned: "Why didn't you come forward sooner?"

- If senior managers and supervisors are involved in sexual harassment or condone the behavior, they are role models for the wrong behavior.

- Often if a woman makes a charge against a man, the issue becomes not the man's behavior but the woman's character, motives, and mental stability.

- If a woman wants to work in some organizations, especially ones that have been traditionally populated with men, the price is defined as putting up with the sex jokes, sexual comments, etc.

- Women feel ambivalent about confronting male mentors who can have enormous influence on their careers and who they probably like and don't want to hurt. Often they also feel that if they spoke up they may hurt the offender's children or spouse, and even the offender.

- Feelings of confusion, shame, or even guilt are common. They may feel they are to blame or are overreacting.

- Feelings of humiliation or embarrassment are also common. Previous experiences may make it too painful to talk about a current experience. Also, victims know they will have to repeat what happened in detail to many people.

- Women may be ignorant of the law and lack faith in the complaint system (believing it will not work in their behalf or that nothing will be done by management).

- Fear of hurting her career or losing her job is a deterrent to reporting sexual harassment.

Activity 2: Typical Responses

1. Present the following chalktalk about typical ways in which women respond to sexual harassment:

    ☞ *Again you may want to connect this information to the information presented in Exercises #5 and #6.*

- Victims of sexual harassment respond to unwelcome comments and behavior in a variety of ways.

- Some may gain weight or wear nondescript clothes and little makeup to try to stop the sexual harassment.

- Some don't trust men anymore, which creates stress in their personal relationships with men.

- Some try to fit in acting like many of the men to try to prevent some of the more severe sexual harassment.

- Some pretend it's not happening to try to keep from feeling the pain.

- Some deny the impact of the behavior—"It didn't bother me."

- Some do nothing—they feel they have to go along to get along.

- Some quit their jobs and sometimes even change career fields.

- Some try to avoid the harasser and places where the harassment tends to occur.

- Some question or blame themselves, depending on their socialization—"What have I done wrong?" or "I shouldn't have worn that dress."

- Some relabel the harasser's behavior and make excuses for him—"He really didn't mean it; it was only a joke."

- Very few will tell someone about the problem or make a formal complaint.

2. Ask participants to share any additional responses they can think of or ask questions they might have.

3. Conclude with the following comment:

- Sexual harassment is an abuse of power intended to discourage women from being in the workplace. Feeling vulnerable and knowing the system is stacked against them keeps many women silent.

VARIATIONS

■ You can conduct this exercise with a group containing only women. Simply eliminate the men's gender group assignment and split the women into smaller groups if the entire group includes more than 12 participants.

■ If the organization you are working with has experienced sexual harassment of males, include reasons why men don't speak up when harassed.

8 A POWER ISSUE

After examining gender power and its relationship to sexual harassment, participants create their vision of a model equal gender-power organization.

GOALS

To recognize the use of power as a part of sexual harassment on the job.

To understand that sexual harassment is based on cultural norms for male and female behavior.

To identify why men harass women and why women don't usually speak up.

GROUP SIZE

20–25 participants.

TIME

2 ½ hours.

MATERIALS

Easel and easel pad; magic markers; masking tape.

PROCESS

Activity 1: Beginning Questions

1. Start out by asking the following questions:

    ✔ Men, what goes on in the minds of men when they harass women?

    ☞ *Many have never thought about this so don't expect a lot of answers.*

    ✔ Women, what are some terms used to label women who claim they have been sexually harassed?

    ☞ *Responses may include "crazy," "bitch," "oversensitive," "a woman scorned," "vengeful," "fantasizing," or the statement "it's all in her mind."*

    ✔ Why do some men engage in sexual harassment?

    ☞ *Tell them you are looking for one word and wait for them to say "power" or "intimidation."*

✔ How do women respond when another woman speaks out about sexual harassment?

☞ *Responses include "Some will not support the women even if they have received the same behavior," "They may back the man and blame the women," and "Why are you hurting this man's career?" (these responses are the result of internalized sexism).*

2. Briefly introduce the exercise with the following points about sexual harassment and power:

- Sexual harassment, like rape, is an abuse of power.

- In a sexually harassing situation, one or more persons impose some type of sexual attention—unwanted and unreturned—on a person or persons who are not in a position to prevent it.

- The harasser consciously or unconsciously uses this unwanted sexual attention to intimidate, control, or embarrass the victim.

- Supervisors and managers have formal organizational power because of their position and may use their power to gain sexual favors.

- Men in general hold informal power simply because our culture has traditionally viewed men as worth more than women, regardless of the position they may hold in any organization and despite the fact that many men feel powerless in their own personal and professional lives.

Activity 2: Gender Power

1. Divide participants into same-gender groups and assign them the following tasks:

➤ The men's group should discuss the following questions and record their responses on easel paper:

➤ Why do men engage in sexual harassment in the workplace—what motivates men to sexually harass women on the job?

➤ Why so some men not harass or hardly ever harass women?

➤ The women's group should discuss the following topics and record their responses on an easel:

➤ Why do women respond to sexual harassment the way they do—usually by not speaking up?

➤ Why do women usually not engage in sexual harassment of men or why might they sexually harass a man?

➤ You have 30 minutes for this task.

2. Move the groups to separate meeting areas and allow them 30 minutes to complete their tasks.

☞ *The male facilitator(s) may have to keep the men on task; they sometimes divert the issue or change the subject.*

3. Reconvene the entire group and, starting with the men, have the groups report their results using the following process:

   a. Ask the men to sit in the center of the room, post their easel chart, and report what they discussed and recorded.

      ☞ *The male facilitator may need to help the men make the following points (these issues should have been discussed in their group, but sometimes men are reluctant to share this information with women):*

      • *Most sexual harassers are exercising their gender power and expect women to remain silent.*

      • *Some men are also trying to bolster their egos, reassuring themselves about their masculinity.*

      • *Men often ignore the impact of sexual harassment, (i.e., "He was only joking"), deny they did anything wrong, or count on their status to protect them; or they may feel the woman "deserved it" because of her dress or actions.*

      • *Men who seldom or never engage in sexual harassment usually like and support women, have explored their own sexism and are willing to continue to examine any sexist behavior. These men usually have some understanding of the impact of men's behavior on women, and some are even willing to risk male rejection by being allies to women.*

   b. Encourage questions from the women after the men have finished.

   c. Repeat the process with the women's group reporting and the men's group asking questions.

4. Summarize what has been discussed and make the following points:

   • Although it is possible that sexual harassment may derive from sexual desire, in most cases it is motivated by fear, the quest for power, and even hatred of women.

   • Many men resent women in the workplace and do not like competing with them.

   • Sexual harassment can also act as an expression of this resentment.

☞ *If you are working with people from traditionally male profes-*
sions, you may also want to mention that sexual harassment
tends to be very high or more intense in these organization as
some men use sexual harassment to try to get women to quit.

- Some psychologists also believe that men who are insecure about their sexuality or status compensate by acting macho—using women to bolster their egos.

- Women tend to not speak up and are motivated to keep quiet out of fear and embarrassment, or because of their socialization, which leaves them feeling they must have done something wrong to receive that kind of behavior.

- Sexual harassment creates an unfair work advantage for men as they don't contend with the same hostility, degradation, and intimidation as women while performing their jobs in a professional manner.

5. Lead a discussion using the following question:

✔ Would you be personally offended to have your spouse, daughter, or mother receive the kind of sexual harassment that typically occurs in your organization?

☞ *Make sure to help the men see that they are often offended if*
a relative is the victim of sexual harassment, but not when the
victim is a woman colleague. Have them attempt to explain the
difference in their responses.

Activity 3: Creating Equal Power Relationships

1. Form mixed-gender groups of 8 participants and give them the following instructions:

➤ Each group has 35 minutes to design an organization in which women and men have equal power relationships.

➤ Consider how the organization's hierarchy would be structured, how decisions would be made, and what would happen (or not happen) both during professional meetings and during informal socializing.

➤ Record the highlights of your discussion on an easel chart.

➤ Don't worry about whether you could actually create a perfect organization—remember, you are creating an ideal.

2. After 35 minutes, reconvene the entire group and have each group report the results of their work.

3. Lead a discussion using the following questions:

   ✔ What elements were common among every group's ideal organization?

   ✔ What would men have to give up and what would they gain in such an organization?

   ✔ Would men have to start seeing all women, not just wives, mothers, or daughters, as persons deserving respect?

   ✔ What would women have to give up and what would they gain in such an organization?

   ✔ How could each of you work toward making this organization more like the ideal you just created?

4. Conclude by making the following points:

   • Sexual harassment has been an easy way for men to try to feel powerful and to keep women in their place.

   • Women have been too willing to "take it" and not demand respect.

   • It will not be easy to use your power to change these dynamics, but I hope you take it as a personal challenge to make a difference and help create a workplace where everyone shares power.

VARIATIONS

■ If you want to make the task more personal, ask the men during Activity 2 to discuss their personal motives or goals when they engage in sexual harassment.

■ Show all or parts of the Anita Hill-Clarence Thomas hearings on the videocassette **Sex and Justice**, available from the Ladyslipper Catalog, 1-800-634-6044.

9 REVERSING THE ROLES

In this highly-interactive exercise, participants reverse gender roles to gain insight about male and female behavior. Use this emotionally-powerful exercise with care.

GOALS

To give participants some insight to male and female behavior during incidents of sexual harassment.

To give men the opportunity to experience the same feelings women encounter when harassed.

To give women the opportunity to feel the gender power men experience in everyday life.

GROUP SIZE

Unlimited.

TIME

3 hours (1 hour for the first activity, 2 hours for the second on the following day).

MATERIALS

Music; refreshments.

PROCESS

☞ *Warning: This exercise can cause participants to experience strong feelings and is not recommended for basic company sexual harassment workshops. It is best utilized with a group of people such as counselors who have participated in many experiential activities in the past. Stress to group members that participation is optional and voluntary.*

Conduct Activity 1 at the end of the first day of a 2- or 3-day workshop. Conduct Activity 2 the next morning. Set the training room up to resemble a social mixer or, ideally, use a hospitality suite.

Activity 1: The Social Scene

1. Briefly introduce the exercise by making the following points:

©1995 Whole Person Press   210 W Michigan Duluth MN 55802   (800) 247-6789

- Participation in this exercise is strictly voluntary and could be uncomfortable for some of you.

- However, if you can get beyond your discomfort, the exercise will provide you with valuable insights about the other gender.

- Today's activity involves a gender-reversal role play—the men will behave as women and the women will behave as men. It lasts about 30 minutes, but we can take more time if you wish.

  ☞ *The more time you allow, the deeper the feelings are likely to become. Use the time to help control the depth and intensity of this exercise.*

- During tomorrow's activity, we will discuss what happened during the role play, so you have overnight to consider your feelings.

- If you don't wish to participate, feel free to leave.

2. After allowing those who wish to leave, divide participants into same-gender groups and give them the following instructions:

  ➤ In a few minutes, we will perform a gender-reversal role play.

  ➤ The scene is a typical company party.

  ➤ Stay in your roles at all times—remember, the men are to behave as women and the women are to behave as men.

  ➤ I want to stress that this does not mean that you are expected to change your gender, just your behavior. Do not change your name or alter the pitch of your voice.

  ☞ *This point is important to make because some men and women try to change their gender. What you want them to experience is only a change in role behavior.*

  ➤ Before the activity begins, you will meet with your facilitators to discuss common gender-role traits you may wish to exhibit during the "party."

  ➤ Feel free to leave any time after 30 minutes. We will discuss what occurred in the morning.

3. Have the male participants meet with the male facilitators and the female participants with the female facilitators to discuss ways they might interact in the exercise.

  ☞ *Have the facilitators give participants suggestions on how to act in ways typical of the gender they will play—how to speak to members of both genders, how to look at members of the other gender, their level of aggressiveness, etc. They are to prepare*

> *participants to experience gender interaction behaving as a member of the opposite sex, so they may be the perpetrators or victims of sexual harassment.*

4. After both groups have prepared, begin the role play "party."

   > ☞ *It is important that you participate and observe the activity. With the tables turned, the group will no doubt encounter some incidents of sexual harassment, which is the goal. Keep a careful watch on how the role play develops and don't let incidents escalate (for example, don't let comments become abusive and do not allow gestures to turn into offensive physical contact). The other facilitators should also participate and make mental notes of what they observe.*

5. When you feel the activity has run its course or more than half of the participants have left, announce that the role play is officially over and remind participants to think about their experience.

Activity 2: What Did We Learn?

1. Form mixed gender groups of 6–8 participants and assign a number and a facilitator to each group.

2. Call each group, in turn, to sit in the center of the room facing each other and use the following questions to discuss their role play experience while the other groups observe:

   ✔ How did you feel about the experience overall?

   ✔ How did you behave and feel as you acted the role of the other gender? What was it like?

   ✔ How did you react to participants of the other gender as they acted the role of your gender? Were they accurate in their portrayal? Why or why not?

   > ☞ *Men often think the women were exaggerating, especially if they get into "hitting on" them in blatant ways. Comments such as this provide an opportunity for the women to share that not only were they not exaggerating, but that, based on their actual experiences with men, they could have been stronger.*

   ✔ When were you feeling powerful? When were you feeling powerless? What contributed to these feelings?

   > ☞ *Women often enter the room feeling powerful and continue to feel in control and the men often feel powerless even though*

some will try to keep control. Some men are used to looking at women's bodies, evaluating them, and then moving on or deciding to "hit on a woman." Their own bodies are not as often subject to evaluation, and that feels very uncomfortable for most men.

✔ How does this experience relate to your own gender experiences as a man or woman in this society?

3. When each group has answered the questions, have them meet in separate places to discuss the following questions:

✔ What would it be like if men and women were to act in equal gender roles? How would it be different? What would we need to change in order for the interactions to be equal?

✔ What insights have you gained from this exercise?

✔ What personal gender-role behavior would you like to commit yourself to changing?

4. Reconvene the entire group and invite participants to share what they plan to change about their own gender-role behavior.

VARIATION

■ If this is only a one day workshop and you want to use this exercise, conduct the entire exercise in the late morning or early afternoon.

10 THE CONTINUUM

In this active exercise, participants move on a continuum to illustrate a discussion of the types of sexual harassment that exist in their organization.

GOALS

To identify types of sexual harassment that exist in today's workplace.

To illustrate how people perceive sexual harassment differently.

GROUP SIZE

Unlimited.

TIME

1 hour.

MATERIALS

Magic markers; **Sexual Harassment Continuum** worksheet.

PROCESS

☞ *Prior to the exercise, create a newsprint continuum chart similar to the one found at the top of the* **Sexual Harassment Continuum** *worksheet, only make it long enough to stretch across one of the room's walls.*

1. Briefly introduce the exercise with the following chalktalk:

   • People perceive sexual harassment in a variety of ways.

   • Sexual harassment is often part of sexual conduct once accepted by society or once tolerated in the workplace.

   • Try to perceive sexual harassment on a continuum ranging from visual and verbal comments to physical touches and assault or even rape—something like this. . . .

      ☞ *Point to the continuum chart on the wall.*

2. Distribute copies of the **Sexual Harassment Continuum** worksheet and review the range of potentially harassing behaviors so participants fully understand the continuum.

3. Distribute the magic markers and ask participants to go to the chart and place a check under each of the categories or behaviors they have witnessed or know have occurred in their organization.

©1995 Whole Person Press   210 W Michigan Duluth MN 55802   (800) 247-6789

☞ *Emphasize that they are to consider the entire organization, not just one department or division.*

4. After they have finished, ask participants to stand by the category they feel is most common to their organization—the behavior they think occurs on a regular basis or they have witnessed most often.

5. Ask participants to look around and see where others are standing.

6. Ask participants to sit down under their category and lead a discussion using the following questions:

   ✔ Without identifying those involved, what specific incidents lead you to select the category you're sitting under?

   ☞ *Even if no one placed a mark or stood under a particular category, that doesn't mean that behavior hasn't or won't occur in the organization, so make sure to mention something about each space.*

   ✔ Considering where you are all sitting, what can we interpret about this organization and sexual harassment?

7. Conclude by asking each participant to finish the following open-ended sentence:

   • To reduce or eliminate the number of sexual harassment incidents here, I can personally . . .

VARIATIONS

■ After *Step 5* present information about the number of incidents reported under each category. This information can usually be obtained from the civil rights or human resource office.

■ If participants are from various organizations, have them put their check marks on a separate line and have each organization stand at the continuum separately.

SEXUAL HARASSMENT CONTINUUM

visual   verbal   physical   assault   rape

Visual
- Pin ups and pornography (including video)
- Graffiti on walls with sexual comments, remarks, and drawings (sometimes about a specific person)
- Cartoons of a sexual nature, sexual magazines and catalogs
- Sexual messages in E-mail
- Letters and cards with sexual messages or pornographic pictures
- Leers and suggestive looks
- Sexually explicit or obscene gestures

Verbal
- Catcalls and whistles
- Sexual or dirty jokes; misogynist humor
- Sexual comments or innuendos about clothing, body, or sexual activities; sexual teasing
- Hostile insults
- Talking about sexual exploits or a partner's sexual inadequacies
- Obscene phone calls

Physical
- Strippers at parties
- Massages
- Unwelcome hugs and long, sexual handshakes
- Kissing
- Patting, pinching, or other inappropriate touching ("accidentally" brushing against someone)
- Touching (especially breasts, hips, and genitals)
- Indecent exposure

Assault
- Grabbing, pinching, cornering, trapping, or blocking someone
- Repeated pressure for dates
- Propositions (implied and overt threats and pressure for sexual favors)
- Forced fondling
- Masturbating or rubbing genitals against someone
- Stalking
- Hitting, physically threatening violence or actual acts of violence

Rape
- Coercive rape
- Assault rape

©1995 Whole Person Press   210 W Michigan Duluth MN 55802   (800) 247-6789

11 WHAT DO YOU THINK ABOUT IT?

Using worksheets and actual harassment case scenarios, participants discuss a range of sexually harassing behavior to gain a better understanding of its many forms.

GOALS

To provide participants an opportunity to discuss specific examples of sexual harassment.

To examine personal reactions to sexually harassing behavior.

To understand the many forms of sexual harassment.

To identify sexual harassment that occurs in the participants' organizations and examine how they can prevent similar incidents from occurring in the future.

GROUP SIZE

Unlimited.

TIME

2–3 hours (depending on the number of participants and the number of examples used).

MATERIALS

Easel and easel pad; magic markers; masking tape; **What Do You Think?** worksheet.

PROCESS

☞ *Prior to the exercise, select a variety of workplace or school/college sexual harassment scenarios, photocopy them, tape each to a sheet of easel paper, and post them around the room. Choose the ones most appropriate to your participants. Mix the scenarios up—don't place all the severe examples next to each other.*

Activity 1: Sexual Harassment Scenarios

1. Introduce the exercise with the following chalktalk:
   • Sexual harassment in organizations comes in many forms.

- Today we will have an opportunity to discuss some of these forms and determine if they occur in your organization.

- We also want to give you an opportunity to discuss ways to handle various types of sexual harassment should they occur in your organization.

2. Provide the following instructions:

  ➤ Around the room I have posted actual sexual harassment scenarios that have been reported in organizations.

  ➤ Walk around the room and quickly read all the scenarios without talking.

3. After about 7 minutes, reconvene the group and distribute copies of the worksheet.

4. Form small groups of 4 participants and give them the following instructions:

  ➤ Each group will be assigned 4 scenarios.

  ➤ As a group, answer the questions on the worksheet for each scenario you are assigned.

  ➤ Record your answers under the appropriate scenarios on the wall.

  ➤ You will have 30 minutes to discuss the scenarios and record your answers, after which you will be asked to report your results to the entire group.

5. Assign each group 4 scenarios, distribute magic markers, and tell them to begin.

  ☞ *For convenience, assign each group scenarios posted next to each other.*

  Have facilitators circulate around the room to listen to discussions and consult with any group that needs clarification of the task. Facilitators should not offer any answers at this point.

6. After 30 minutes, call time and use the following process to allow each group to report their results and discuss the examples:

  a. Select a group to read its first scenario and share its responses to the worksheet questions.

  b. Invite the other participants to react to and ask questions regarding the group's responses.

    ☞ *Encourage participants to share any times when they have participated in, observed, or heard about similar incidents.*

> *The exercise becomes more meaningful if you can create a safe enough environment for any of the women to share their own experiences with sexual harassment. No one, however, should ever be forced to share.*

   c. Repeat *Steps a* and *b* until the group has covered all its scenarios.

   d. Repeat the process with another group until each group has reported their replies to all their scenarios.

7. When all the groups have reported, thank the group members for their participation and invite them to share any other observations, reactions, or feelings they experienced during the exercise.

VARIATIONS

■ If you are working with only one organization, choose examples for the group that you know have occurred in that organization (if you have access to that knowledge) and tell them that all the scenarios were reported to have occurred in their organization. Add any to the list that you believe are significant for the organization you are working with.

■ If your time is limited, you may not be able to engage in an in-depth discussion of all the examples. Provide time for each group to at least read each of their scenarios and share their major points.

■ Instead of having one group go through all its examples and then moving on to another group, have a group share only one example and discuss it and then move on to the next group, etc. After one round, go back to the first group. Continue until you have covered all the examples.

Workplace Sexual Harassment Scenarios

1. A woman has to make client visits with a male colleague. Every time they go out on their visits, he makes comments about her body and what he'd like to do to her.

2. A male supervisor walks into a woman's office in another division and proceeds to tell her about a business trip he took recently and how he engaged in a *menage a trois*. She is alone in her office with this man and has never met him before this discussion.

3. A woman and man are friends and colleagues. They even socialize outside of work. One day, out of the blue, the man tells the woman that when he is having sex with his wife, he is actually fantasizing about being with her, not his wife. He tells her this as they are about to enter a critical sales meeting with a client.

4. Men pass a copy of *Playboy* magazine around the office and discuss parts of it during breaks. The women in the office observe this taking place.

5. A woman has been turned down for a promotion and is passed over for career-enhancing business trips in favor of a woman who is having an affair with the manager. There has been a pattern of this manager sleeping with women in his office and then promoting them.

6. When meeting with a female subordinate, a male supervisor often makes remarks like: "You have great legs; you should wear short skirts more often," and "I didn't hear a word you said at today's staff meeting because of the way you filled out that red dress." He does not give her any feedback about her work, even when she requests it.

7. A high level manager (a man) from headquarters asks to meet a mid level manager (a woman) who is in town to review a key project. He says he is unavailable during the day but suggests meeting her for dinner. They agree to meet in her hotel lobby at 7 P.M., but he knocks on her hotel room door at 6:30 P.M. even though she has not given him her room number. When she opens the door, he pushes his way in and tries to kiss and fondle her, suggesting they order room service.

8. A female supervisor finds the office secretary crying in the rest room. Upon probing, the secretary says that their boss has just shown her an explicit sexual computer program. The secretary is so upset she decides to take the rest of the day off. Their boss asks the supervisor what's wrong with the secretary, and she tells him. He replies, "That was nothing, she's just an uptight old maid," and proceeds to show the female supervisor the same computer program.

9. There is a joke that some men like to play on a new woman employee at the plant. The men on the crew surround the woman and one of them says "I bet you one dollar I can make your breasts wiggle without touching you." The pressure is so great to be a good sport that the woman usually accepts the wager. The man then grabs her breasts and tells her she can keep the dollar.

10. A female assistant must walk through a plant to deliver mail to the supervisor every day. Each time she hears comments about her "ass," how she moves, her bra size, and even catcalls and whistles.

11. During a slow period at work, peers tell and laugh at sex jokes, except for one woman and one man. A typical joke: "What's the difference between excess and surplus? Excess is what you can't get in your mouth. Surplus is the other tit."

12. A supervisor brings a lingerie catalog to work and asks his secretary to look through it and pick something out to give his wife on Valentine's Day that will liven up their sex life.

13. When having a conversation with the women in the office, a male colleague talks to their breasts and tries to brush up against them in an "innocent" way.

14. A group of professional peers go out to lunch while in New York City for a conference. One of the men asks a woman peer if she would like to taste his ice cream cone. She says "no," to which he replies, "Oh, come on. Why don't you lick it? I bet you can lick it real good."

15. Some men are standing around in the office hallway discussing the physical attributes of the women who walk by. As one woman passes by they mention how they would like to "get into her pants" loud enough so she can hear it.

16. A sales meeting presenter tells off-color jokes and shows a few scenes from pornographic movies as part of his sales motivating speech to all of the company's sales staff, which includes both women and men.

17. A woman trainee finds a birthday present wrapped on her desk from the men in her office. She opens it up and finds a vibrator in the shape of a penis.

18. A man and a woman are on an elevator. He starts to make comments about her body and moves closer to her, making more graphic remarks the closer he gets.

©1995 Whole Person Press   210 W Michigan Duluth MN 55802   (800) 247-6789

19. A woman secretary has to work late one evening at the office to finish a report for her boss. All of a sudden she hears a noise and finds a supervisor from another division has his penis out and is starting to rub it against her back.

20. A man drops his report on the floor and as he kneels to pick it up, another man in the meeting (there are only men present) says: "While you're down there . . ."

21. A male supervisor asks a female staff member out on a date. Although she refuses, he continues to ask.

22. At staff meetings, a manager frequently sits next to a woman employee. He occasionally touches her arm and rubs her neck.

23. A group of men paste nude photos from *Playboy* onto biographies of new women employees that the company includes in its newsletter.

24. A woman walks past a group of men in the hall of the office. One of the men pulls her over and says to her: "I have a stiff proposition, if you have an opening." The men all laugh.

College/School Sexual Harassment Scenarios

1. A teacher jokes in class as he asks a female student to turn off the lights to see a slide show, saying, "Women do their best work in the dark."

2. A male professor asks a married woman in his psychology class how her husband is in bed and offers his services if she feels frustrated.

3. A male professor asks a female student out on a date. She turns him down, saying she has to study that night for his test. He tells her he will take care of the test and not to worry about it.

4. A woman is a senior at a small college, an "A" student who has earned praise from her professors. She expects to go on to graduate school. A professor, the chairperson of the department she is majoring in, propositions her one day, and she turns him down. She needs his recommendation for graduate school and under his continued pressure to go to bed with him, she agrees.

5. A medical school professor uses pornography to spice up his lectures, often calls women "babes" and "dolls," and always refers to doctors as "he."

6. In a high school, young women receive sexual comments from young men as they walk through the halls. They are often rated as to their sexual attractiveness and several of the males have even "mooned" the women.

©1995 Whole Person Press   210 W Michigan Duluth MN 55802   (800) 247-6789

WHAT DO YOU THINK?

Directions: Discuss each sexual harassment scenario using the questions below and record your answers on the easel sheet accompanying the appropriate scenario.

1. How often do you think this type of sexual harassment occurs in your organization?

   Never   Rarely   Sometimes   Often   Every day

2. How would you rate this case of sexual harassment?

   Subtle/ambiguous   Moderate   Severe

3. What could be the possible intent of the harasser(s)?

4. How do you think the target of the harassment feels?

5. How do you think the target would respond in your organization?

6. What do you think is the best way for the target to handle this situation?

7. How would most managers or supervisors of the harasser typically handle this situation in your organization?

8. What do you think supervisors should do in this situation?

9. What should the penalty of the harasser be?

Considering
Consequences

CONSIDERING CONSEQUENCES

12 TAKING ON THE BOYS' CLUB (p 71)

Using a survey and a video, participants explore the risks and benefits of confronting discrimination and sexual harassment. (2 hours)

13 TRUE STORIES (p 74)

In the safety of same-gender groups, women share their experiences with sexual harassment. Women tell their male colleagues how they have been harassed in the workplace so the men can confront any denial they may harbor and become motivated to help end harassment in their organization. (2 ½ hours)

14 POWER AND THE WORKPLACE (p 79)

Using a video depicting examples of sexual harassment, participants discuss and analyze various forms of unwelcome behavior in the workplace. (2 ½ hours)

15 SEXUAL HARASSMENT IMPACT (p 84)

By identifying the incredible personal and financial costs of sexual harassment, participants become motivated to help make their workplace free of unwelcome behavior. (1 hour)

12 TAKING ON THE BOYS' CLUB

Using a survey and a video, participants explore the risks and benefits of confronting discrimination and sexual harassment.

GOALS

To understand how sexual harassment and discrimination function in organizations.

To examine how women can risk taking a stand against discriminatory behavior.

To identify some dynamics of sexism that most women will experience in the workplace.

GROUP SIZE

Up to 30 participants.

TIME

2 hours.

MATERIALS

Note cards; easel and easel pad; magic markers; masking tape; pencils and pens; TV and VCR; **Taking on the Boys Club** videocassette (available from Coronet/MTI Film & Video, 1-800-777-2400).

PROCESS

☞ *This exercise works particularly well with women and men in supervisory and managerial positions.*

Activity 1: Opening Survey

1. Distribute note cards to each participant and give them the following instructions:

   ➤ Write "sexual discrimination" at the top of one side and "sexual harassment" at the top of the other.

   ➤ On the sexual discrimination side, write several examples of sexual discrimination you have witnessed in your organization. The examples do not have to be anything you personally experienced.

➤ On the same side, rate how much of a problem you think sexual discrimination is in your organization. Use a scale of 1 to 10 where 1 means "no problem" and 10 means "severe problem."

➤ On the sexual harassment side, write several examples of sexual harassment you have witnessed in your company. Again, the examples do not have to be anything you personally experienced.

➤ Use the same scale to rate how much of a problem you think sexual harassment is in your organization.

➤ Do not put your name on the card.

☞ *Write a summary of the instructions on an easel sheet prior to the exercise so participants can refer to them.*

2. When most have finished, collect the cards, shuffle them, and redistribute them so each participant has someone else's card.

3. Have each participant read the sexual discrimination examples from their cards and summarize the examples on an easel.

4. Have each participant read the sexual discrimination severity ranking on their cards and record them on an easel chart prepared with a scale from 1 to 10.

5. Repeat *Steps 3* and *4* having participants read from the sexual harassment side of their cards.

Activity 2: Risks and Payoffs of Confrontation

1. Introduce the video with the following chalktalk:

   • We are now going to watch **Taking on the Boys Club**, a video that demonstrates the ways sexual harassment and sexual discrimination can keep women from enjoying equality in the workplace.

   • It shows how 2 women—a neurosurgeon and a lawyer—have handled sexual harassment and sexual discrimination in their workplaces.

2. Show the video (it lasts about 15 minutes).

3. Form mixed-gender groups of 6–8 participants, have each move to separate spaces with an easel, and give them the following instructions:

   ➤ You are to develop 2 lists:

   ➤ One should include the possible risks of confronting sexual discrimination and harassment in the organization.

➤ The other should include possible benefits of confronting sexual discrimination and harassment in the organization.

☞ *Write a summary of the instructions on an easel sheet prior to the exercise so participants can refer to them.*

4. After 20 minutes, reconvene the entire group and have each group read their lists (begin with confrontation risks).

5. Ask for volunteers to share examples of when they confronted sexual harassment or discrimination or were an ally to someone who did.

☞ *Ask them to describe what happened. If no one has any examples, discuss what this may say about their organizational climate— either no one has been harassed or discriminated against or, more likely, employees fear retaliation.*

6. Conclude by encouraging participants to help create a positive climate in their organization by taking risks to eliminate sexual discrimination and harassment.

VARIATIONS

■ If you are short on time, eliminate Activity 1.

■ In *Step 3* of Activity 2, form same-gender groups and then lead a discussion about gender perception by comparing their lists following *Step 4*.

©1995 Whole Person Press   210 W Michigan Duluth MN 55802   (800) 247-6789

13 TRUE STORIES

In the safety of same-gender groups, women share their experiences with sexual harassment. Women tell their male colleagues how they have been harassed in the workplace so the men can confront any denial they may harbor and become motivated to help end harassment in their organization.

GOALS

To provide participants with an opportunity to share their sexual harassment experiences with members of their own gender.

To empower women to speak up about sexual harassment.

To allow men to confront their denial of the sexual harassment they or their colleagues may be guilty of.

To motivate participants to prevent and stop workplace sexual harassment.

GROUP SIZE

Up to 25 participants (including at least 6 women).

TIME

2 ½ hours.

MATERIALS

None.

PROCESS

☞ *Caution: This exercise can become quite intense.*

Activity 1: Gender Sharing

1. Introduce the exercise with the following chalktalk:
   - ✔ We are going to examine examples of sexual harassment in this organization.
   - ✔ To get the most out of the activity, everyone must be open and honest.
   - ✔ We must also all remember to remain confidential—nothing mentioned in this exercise is to be repeated outside this forum.

2. Divide participants into same-gender groups and move them to separate rooms accompanied by facilitators of the appropriate gender.

3. Have the facilitators of the women's group conduct the activity using the following process:

   a. Explain that participants will have an opportunity to discuss sexual harassment they have experienced in the workplace.

   b. Present some ground rules for this session, such as:

      • Honor confidentiality. No one should share or discuss what anyone else said in the group. It is okay to discuss anything you personally shared.

      • Avoid interrupting when someone is sharing an experience.

      • Be attentive and support each other.

      • Sharing is voluntary.

   c. Give each woman an opportunity to share her experiences with sexual harassment.

      ☞ *Do not place pressure on anyone to share personal experiences. For most women, sharing is cathartic and relieving, but a few may not be ready to share because reliving the experience will be too painful or because they tend not to talk about anything personal. Encourage them to avoid self-blame.*

   d. Lead them, when appropriate, to explore ways they can deal with harassment or try to prevent it.

      ☞ *A discussion about sexual harassment may trigger a memory, and at times you may find that a woman or many women (one woman's sharing may also trigger the memories of other women) will share a non-work situation, such as rape or sexual abuse. If this occurs, it is very important that they feel supported by the group—listen to their experiences and feelings and always remind them the assault was not their fault. After the exercise, a female facilitator should individually speak with each woman who shared a non-work abuse experience. Ask her how she feels after having shared this information (sometimes it is the first time) and give her information about counseling and support resources in her community. Recovery usually takes time, and recalling the memory or talking about it are only the first steps in a healing process.*

4. Have the facilitators of the men's group conduct the activity using the following process:

a. Explain that participants will have an opportunity to openly discuss sexual harassment with other men.

b. Provide some ground rules, such as:

- Always speak for yourself, using "I" messages.

- Honor confidentiality. No one should share or discuss what anyone else said in the group. It is okay to discuss anything you personally shared.

- Avoid using rationalizations for male behavior.

- Stay focused on the issue at hand.

c. Provide the following instructions:

➤ Each of you will have an opportunity to share examples of times when you have participated in sexual harassment in the workplace.

➤ You will also discuss times when you have observed sexual harassment and have done nothing about it as well as times when you have done something about it.

➤ Finally, you will have time to share examples of when you have been the target of sexual harassment. (Optional)

☞ *Keep in mind that some men may deny that they have ever participated in or seen much sexual harassment in their work environment. This is normal (most people experience denial about actions they are not proud of). It is important that the male facilitators share their own experiences—modeling openness and confronting the male participants with what is actually happening in their own workplace. The ground rules will set the framework. However, men may divert the issue by focusing on how threatened they feel with the new emphasis on sexual harassment and discuss their fear that women will use the law against them. Or they may want to spend their energies on how women bring sexual harassment on themselves by how they dress. They may also use rationalizations such as, "There is nothing wrong with a little good-natured kidding," "People should have freedom of speech," or "I shouldn't have to change my behavior just because of one or two people."*

This time with the men can be very frustrating for the male facilitators because individuals who haven't seen or experienced the negative results of sexual harassment may have difficulty perceiving or accepting the problem. Keep the men focused on the issues.

5. After about an hour, facilitators from both gender groups should meet and discuss what has occurred in their groups and make any necessary adjustments for Activity 2.

6. Have the women facilitators share the following information with their group before reconvening with the men:

   - In the next activity, we will have an opportunity to share with the men some of the sexual harassment examples we just discussed.

   - It is important that men understand the impact of sexual harassment.

   - Sharing this information in past workshops has helped some men understand how hurtful their actions can be—something many men do not realize.

   - The more people understand about the impact of harassing behavior, the better the chance they will help prevent or stop it.

   - Sharing your experiences is completely voluntary. Make sure to let me know if you do not wish to explain your experiences.

     ☞ *It is critical to ask them if they are willing to participate and how they feel about sharing with the men. If a woman chooses not to share anything ask her if she will sit with the group to give the rest of the women support.*

7. Have the men facilitators share the following information with their group before reconvening with the women:

   - The women are going to tell us about some of their experiences with sexual harassment in the workplace.

   - Remember that everything shared in this activity is confidential— in fact, part of the activity involves pledging your commitment to honor confidentiality.

   - Be sure to listen and do not interrupt while they are speaking.

   - After the women have finished, you will be asked to share your own feelings and reactions to what you heard.

Activity 2: Fishbowl

1. Reconvene the entire group and have the woman sit in the center of the room on pillows (or chairs) facing each other.

   ☞ *It is more effective to have the women sit on pillows in the center. The men can hear better and chairs have a barrier effect. However, do not let this become an issue; if women object to the floor let them sit in chairs.*

©1995 Whole Person Press   210 W Michigan Duluth MN 55802   (800) 247-6789

2. Have each of the participants take the following pledge of confidentiality:

- I promise not to repeat anything that someone else says during this activity.

    ☞ *Some participants may feel self-conscious taking a pledge, but remind them of the sensitive nature of sharing these experiences and the importance of having everyone feel comfortable during the discussion. Taking the pledge promotes honesty.*

3. Have the women take turns sharing examples of times when they have been sexually harassed and the impact harassment has had on them.

    ☞ *It is usually helpful to have a woman facilitator share first, unless a woman participant starts talking right away. Facilitators also should provide support whenever necessary.*

4. Ask the men to change places with the women and share their feelings about what they heard and the impact on them personally, especially in terms of experiences that resemble their own behavior.

    ☞ *A male facilitator should begin, acting as a model of how to respond. It is important that the men share personal feelings and not talk about the issue or play the role of rescuer at this point. Every man should be encouraged to say what he is feeling. Facilitators may need to help the men share their feelings because some men find it difficult to identify and share the feelings they experience while listening to the women.*

5. When all the men have shared, allow time for the women to share their reactions to the men's responses.

6. Lead an open discussion with the entire group about any unfinished issues and how the men might help to stop or prevent sexual harassment now that they realize its impact.

7. End this activity by thanking the group for taking risks so all could learn.

©1995 Whole Person Press   210 W Michigan Duluth MN 55802   (800) 247-6789

14 POWER AND THE WORKPLACE

Using a video depicting examples of sexual harassment, participants discuss and analyze various forms of unwelcome behavior in the workplace.

GOALS

To understand the power dynamics of workplace sexual harassment.

To better understand the many different forms sexual harassment can take on the job.

GROUP SIZE

Unlimited.

TIME

2 $1/2$ hours.

MATERIALS

TV and VCR; **Sex, Power, and the Workplace** videocassette (available from KCET Video, 1-800-343-4727).

PROCESS

1. Introduce the exercise with the following chalktalk:

   • Women have been sexually harassed on the job ever since they became part of the work force.

   • Until 1980, however, sexual harassment was unrecognized and, even in the early 1990s, ignored for the most part.

   • The issue exploded with the Anita Hill-Clarence Thomas hearings, which raised many questions: What is sexual harassment? Who's to blame for harassing behavior? Why does it happen? What can be done to prevent it?

   • In today's exercise, we will watch and discuss a video that attempts to answer these questions by presenting examples of workplace sexual harassment.

   • The first example involves Jackie Morris, a woman who works with the American National Can Company in a job traditionally performed by men.

2. Play the video until the end of the Jackie Morris segment, then lead a discussion using the following questions:

    ✔ What kinds of sexual harassment did Jackie experience?

    ✔ What impact did the harassment have on Jackie?

    ✔ Jackie's lawyer said that management's lenient attitude toward sexual harassment perpetuated it. Do you agree?

    ✔ Have you witnessed any similar examples in your own workplace?

3. Introduce the next example by explaining that it shows more subtle forms of sexual harassment experienced by Dr. Frances Conley, a neurosurgeon.

4. Play the video until the end of the Frances Conley segment (after the woman consultant speaks), then lead a discussion using the following questions:

    ✔ Frances endured sexual harassment for over twenty years, believing that if she wanted to be a neurosurgeon, she would have to put up with such behavior. Do you think this is typical of many women's experiences—that they put up with unwanted and unwelcome sexual attention?

    ✔ Education or a high position in an organization don't make sexual harassment go away—they only make it more subtle. What kinds of harassment did Frances experience? Are they similar to ones you have seen in your organization? Is this a power issue?

    ✔ What impact did the long-term sexual harassment have on Dr. Conley?

    ✔ Dr. Conley was constantly reminded of her inferior status because of her gender. Have any of the women in this group questioned yourselves and found your confidence drop as a result of sexual harassment on the job?

    ✔ When women have been silent for a long time about their sexual harassing experiences and then an incident causes them to speak up, how do other people tend to respond?

    ✔ When women keep silent, are they helping to perpetuate a hostile environment?

    ✔ What do you think of the penalty given to the man who became Frances' boss after the sexual harassment investigation? Would such action from management occur in your organization? Why or why not?

5. Introduce and show the segment about the harassment of Kerry Ellison, who worked for the Internal Revenue Service, then lead a discussion using the following questions:

✔ Kerry said "no" to subtle, flirtatious behavior some see as innocent, and expected her harasser to listen to her and stop his actions toward her. Why don't some men stop when women say "no"?

✔ Kerry became concerned for her personal safety after the harassment escalated to a personal letter. Men and women often perceive this kind of behavior differently. Why?

☞ *If it doesn't come up in the discussion, point out that because women are often victims of sexual assault and rape, they are understandably worried whether a harasser's conduct is a prelude to violent sexual assault, whereas men are seldom victims of such attacks and do not see the behavior in the same context.*

✔ Kerry said all she wanted was to be able to come to work and do her job, and that she deserved to be protected against sexual harassment. Do you agree?

✔ The supervisors did not respond as if the situation was serious, and although they temporarily transferred the harasser, they seemed to support him and not her. Even the judge called the case isolated and trivial. What do you think should be the responsibility of supervisors in cases like these?

✔ Kerry's appeal led to a new interpretation of the law, the Reasonable Woman Standard. This means that the conduct should be examined from the viewpoint of the woman. Men and women often perceive the same behavior very differently. Have any of you experienced similar examples of different perceptions concerning harassing behavior?

✔ Some men worry that they will be vulnerable to false accusations. Is this a realistic fear?

6. Explain that the next segment of the video involves a research study of the social dynamics of harassment. Show that portion, and lead a discussion using the following questions:

✔ The study found that men who are highly prone to engage in sexually harassing behavior often find it difficult to understand the perspectives of others, so women's perspectives are probably very alien to them. Do you think this is true of those who sexually harass others in your organization?

©1995 Whole Person Press   210 W Michigan Duluth MN 55802   (800) 247-6789

✔ Is the example of supervisors or managers important in setting either a permissive or professional tone for the working environment? What tone has been set in your company?

✔ The video stated that when extreme sexual harassment occurs in an organization, it is because management has allowed it to occur. Do you agree? What is your responsibility as a supervisor or a manager in your company? (If you are not in management, what do you expect from your manager or supervisor)?

✔ One study found that at least fifty percent of all working women have experienced sexual harassment; others have found that number to be even higher. What do you think the percentage is in your organization? How did you arrive at this number? How could you find out if you have a problem in your company?

7. Explain that the next segment describes how Patricia Kiss, a real estate specialist with the District of Columbia, experienced *quid pro quo* harassment—pressure to exchange sexual favors for workplace benefits—then show the segment and lead a discussion using the following questions:

✔ What labels have women been given when they reject men's advances, as Patricia did at first? What is the intent of men when they say these things to a woman?

✔ How did Patricia's supervisor use his organizational power? What have other supervisors or men done to show women that they have power?

✔ Why are women like Patricia reluctant to report this behavior? When they do report it, what kinds of responses do they tend to get from supervisors in your organization?

> ☞ *The video points out that if women speak out about verbal harassment, they are often asked "Why are you complaining about that?" Complaints of more intense and physical behavior often receive comments such as "Why didn't you say something sooner?"*

✔ What does society need to change about its perceptions of men and women to eliminate sexual harassment?

8. Explain that the remaining segment explains the harassment experienced by Brenda Berkman, a fire fighter in New York City. It also presents an excellent role model for managers, Bob Simmons, a supervisory waterworks engineer.

©1995 Whole Person Press   210 W Michigan Duluth MN 55802   (800) 247-6789

9. Ask participants to note Simmons's positive actions, show the remaining segment, and lead a discussion using the following questions:

✔ What kinds of harassment did Brenda experience? Have you ever witnessed or experienced similar harassment?

✔ What will help men in power stop abusing and using their authority?

✔ Many employees are confused as to what constitutes appropriate behavior. Part of this confusion is the result of our socialization— what society has taught us about how we should behave as women and men. What messages did you receive that may have contributed to how you respond to sexual harassment?

> ☞ *You might want to remind them of the quote from the attorney, Dan Stormer: "Until men start listening to the 'no' and accepting the 'no' as 'no' there are going to be claims of sexual harassment—rightful claims."*

✔ Bob Simmons is an excellent role model of someone who helps create a harassment-free workplace. What positive actions did he take? How was the training session positive? Have you seen similar behavior from supervisors in your organization?

✔ What can women do to help create a harassment-free work environment? What can men do?

10. Conclude with the following chalktalk:

• Hopefully this video and discussion has raised your consciousness about sexual harassment.

• I want to encourage you to become more sensitive to others' responses to your behavior.

• Be open to examining your own behavior and ask yourself if your behavior during the last several years could be perceived as harassment. Examine how you can speak out more clearly so that you do not welcome certain behavior.

• Support each other as you work to change your perceptions and behavior—it will help men and women become true friends and equal partners in the workplace.

VARIATION

■ If you are short on time, only show the segments appropriate for your group, or order the shorter (32 minute) version of the video (available from Excellence in Training Corporation, 1-800-747-6569, or Lumina Productions, 1-800-929-4323).

15 SEXUAL HARASSMENT IMPACT

By identifying the incredible personal and financial costs of sexual harassment, participants become motivated to help make their workplace free of unwelcome behavior.

GOALS

To understand the negative impacts—personal, professional, and organizational—of sexual harassment.

To motivate participants to help create a work environment free of sexual harassment.

GROUP SIZE

Up to 30 participants.

TIME

1 hour.

MATERIALS

Easel and easel pad; magic markers; masking tape; **Impact of Sexual Harassment** worksheets.

PROCESS

1. Introduce the exercise with the following chalktalk:

   • This exercise is designed to help us explore the impact of sexual harassment.

   • The consequences of sexual harassment can be very serious for both the organization and individual employees.

   • Sexual harassment comes with high costs—both personal and financial—to everyone involved.

2. Form mixed-gender groups of 7–8 participants and provide the following instructions:

   ➤ Discuss and identify every possible benefit and cost sexual harassment has on:

   ➣ Targets of the harassing behavior

   ➣ The harasser

©1995 Whole Person Press   210 W Michigan Duluth MN 55802   (800) 247-6789

➤ Witnesses to the harassment

➤ The manager or supervisor of the harasser

➤ The organization

☞ *Write the above list on an easel sheet so the groups can refer to it.*

➤ Make sure to list every possible benefit you see groups gaining from sexual harassment.

➤ Also list every possible cost which may occur as a result of sexual harassment.

➤ You will have 35 minutes for this task.

3. After 35 minutes, reconvene the entire group and discuss their work using the following process:

   a. Have one group report its list of benefits and costs for the first category, targets of the harassing behavior.

   b. Ask the other groups to add any items they discussed that did not appear on the reporting group's list.

   ☞ *Add any items missed by all the groups. See the worksheet for a comprehensive list.*

   c. Repeat *Steps a* and *b,* alternating reporting groups until each category has been discussed; end with the costs and benefits to the organization.

4. Invite participants to make summary statements or generalizations about the costs of sexual harassment based on the lists they created in *Steps 2* and *3.*

   ☞ *Very few benefits, if any, will be identified. Most groups will see the serious consequences of tolerating or allowing sexual harassment in their organization.*

5. Distribute the worksheets and close the exercise with the following chalktalk:

   ☞ *Make sure to tailor the information to your group.*

   • We have just identified many negative consequences of allowing a work environment to contain sexual harassment. The handout you just received contains a complete list of the costs.

   • The most serious consequences are often in work environments that traditionally have been seen as "male" occupations; women often find this work environment filled with highly-violent and intimidating harassment.

- Women in sexually-harassing environments face a no-win situation: if they don't complain about the harassment, it reinforces the notion that women are sex objects and shouldn't be in the work force; if they do object, they are often labeled "complainer"—someone who can't take the heat and who is, therefore, not promotable.

- More and more courts are holding employers responsible for acts of sexual harassment, even when they had no knowledge of what was taking place. Management must take an aggressive stance and immediate and appropriate action when sexual harassment comes to its attention.

- Hopefully this session has enlightened you and encouraged you to take positive action to help prevent and stop sexual harassment in your organization.

VARIATION

■ In *Step 2*, form same-gender groups instead of mixed-gender groups, then examine any differences in the lists of costs and benefits.

©1995 Whole Person Press   210 W Michigan Duluth MN 55802   (800) 247-6789

IMPACT OF SEXUAL HARASSMENT

Target of the Harassment

1. Economic or Job Connected Injuries.

   - Loss of job. Some victims are fired for not giving in to sexual demands. Others find themselves in a situation so intolerable they feel compelled to quit.

   - Poor job performance reviews. Victims may be rated low as punishment for refusing a sexual request or for reporting harassment. Or performance may actually go down because of the time and energy spent dealing with the harassment or the trauma it incurs.

   - Loss of wages and other benefits. Victims are often demoted or denied a promotion or raise because they object to or don't go along with harassment. This in turn impacts pension, vacation pay, bonuses, overtime pay, etc. If they quit or are fired, victims lose medical benefits and pensions and may have difficulty finding another job or may feel forced to take a job at lower pay.

   - Forced transfer. Victims are often transferred to another department while the harasser remains.

   - Additional financial costs. Attorney fees, medical (including counseling), etc.

2. Personal Injuries

   - Emotional stress. Victims often suffer lowered self-esteem or confidence. Targets may begin to question their own self worth, both personally and professionally. They may even blame themselves and think they should have been able to stop the offender. They also experience strained personal relationships with their partner, friends, and family members. Depression often occurs.

   - Physical stress. Victims may experience headaches, nervous tension, sleep and eating disorders, and other stress-related illnesses as the direct result of sexual harassment.

   - Other physical and mental injuries. Physical pranks or violent acts directed at the harassed person can lead to a variety of other injuries.

©1995 Whole Person Press   210 W Michigan Duluth MN 55802   (800) 247-6789

IMPACT OF SEXUAL HARASSMENT, continued

Harasser

1. Career or job loss. Harassers face disciplinary action from the organization. Job possibilities in other organizations could be reduced if their reputation is damaged.

2. Legal liabilities. Harassers may also be legally liable to pay court costs, attorney fees, and damages.

3. Negative interpersonal relationship with colleagues and upper management. Other members of the organization may grow to resent a harasser.

Witnesses to the Harassment

1. Low morale. Observers may suffer a lack of trust in management and reduced loyalty. The organization is seen as an unpleasant place to work.

2. Anxiety, frustration, and embarrassment. Observers wonder if they will be the next victim or what their responsibility is regarding the harassment they have witnessed.

3. Loss of job opportunities. Observers worry that promotions, special assignments, etc., will go to persons who give in to sexual demands and not to those who deserve them.

Manager/Supervisor of the Harasser

1. Lowered performance. Supervisors have to take time out of the daily business to deal with a sexual harassment problem. If not handled correctly, it could impact promotions and other prospects. Employee performance may also suffer because of time and energy spent dealing with the harassment.

2. Lowered morale. Supervisors may experience loss of respect from their employees and colleagues if they do not deal effectively with sexual harassment.

3. Court action and investigations. A sexual harassment investigation may uncover many other problems in a supervisor's department.

©1995 Whole Person Press   210 W Michigan Duluth MN 55802   (800) 247-6789

IMPACT OF SEXUAL HARASSMENT, continued

Organization

1. Lower productivity. Sexual harassment cases often reduce productivity and teamwork, including the loss of ideas from women—all of which impact the bottom line.

2. Lower morale and reduced employee loyalty.

3. Increased absenteeism and higher medical bills.

4. Increased job turnover and its associated costs in recruitment, hiring, and training. (A *Working Women* magazine survey published in December, 1988, found a typical Fortune 500 company with 23,750 employees loses $6.7 million a year from sexual harassment in absenteeism, low morale, low productivity, and employee turnover. This does not include lawsuits.)

5. Legal costs. Organizations are responsible for fees covering attorneys, court costs, and settlements.

6. Tarnished public image. Sexual harassment cases are often accompanied by negative publicity.

7. Other loss of income. Government and other organizations often cancel contracts with companies that have a sexual harassment problem.

©1995 Whole Person Press   210 W Michigan Duluth MN 55802   (800) 247-6789

TRAINER'S NOTES

Preventing
Harassment

PREVENTING HARASSMENT

16 SETTING THE TONE (p 93)

Designed for supervisors and managers, this exercise allows participants to examine their organizations' sexual harassment policies and informal practices in order to create a better workplace. ($1\frac{1}{2}$ hours)

17 CREATING A POLICY (p 98)

This exercise, which works best with top level managers and committees who make or recommend policy, helps members of organizations create a strong, effective policy to prevent and handle sexual harassment. (2 hours)

18 SPEAKING UP (p 103)

Participants use role playing to practice effective skills for confronting sexual harassment—works well in mixed-gender groups or when only women attend. (3 hours)

19 WORKPLACE RESPONSIBILITIES (p 112)

Using video vignettes of workplace harassment, participants explore how supervisors, witnesses, and targets can stop and prevent sexual harassment. (1 hour)

20 MANAGING INTIMACY (p 119)

Participants discuss the risks and benefits of intimate relationships in the workplace and develop a sexual code of ethics for the organization—an excellent exercise for senior level managers and executives. (2 hours)

16 SETTING THE TONE

Designed for supervisors and managers, this exercise allows participants to examine their organizations' sexual harassment policies and informal practices in order to create a better workplace.

GOALS

To examine how to create a safe and comfortable work environment, free of intimidation and fear.

To identify participants' individual commitment to the elimination and prevention of sexual harassment.

GROUP SIZE

Up to 30 participants.

TIME

$1\frac{1}{2}$ hours.

MATERIALS

Easel and easel pad; magic markers; **Sexual Harassment Policy** worksheet; **Establishing a Harassment-Free Workplace** worksheet.

☞ *It would be helpful to have copies of each participant's company's sexual harassment policy (if the companies have one).*

PROCESS

Activity 1: Our Policy Is . . .

1. Distribute copies of the **Sexual Harassment Policy** worksheet and allow participants 5 minutes to fill it out.

   ☞ *Some participants may not know their organization's policy. Emphasize that no manager or supervisor can afford **not** to know the policy and not to be able to communicate it effectively.*

2. Form small groups of about 8 participants, assign a facilitator to each, and have them discuss their worksheets using the following questions:

   ✔ If you answered part "a" of number one, how did you complete the open-ended sentence?

©1995 Whole Person Press   210 W Michigan Duluth MN 55802   (800) 247-6789

✔ If you answered part "b" of number one, how did you complete the open-ended sentence?

☞ *If participants do not know their organization's policy and you were able to get a copy of it ahead of time, share it with them or give them a copy of it. In any case, make sure they find out what the policy is as soon as possible.*

✔ How can you effectively communicate your company's policy to your employees?

☞ *Record this information on an easel chart.*

Activity 2: Being a Role Model

1. Have participants remain in their small groups and ask facilitators to lead a discussion using the following questions about being a role model for others in their company to help create a sexual harassment-free workplace:

✔ Have you ever been in a situation where you witnessed a higher level manager engage in possible sexually harassing behavior? If so, what impact did it have on you and others in the organization?

✔ Have you ever been in a situation where you saw or heard a higher level manager prevent or stop sexual harassment? What did they do? What impact did their actions have? What message did they convey?

✔ What informal attitude does your organization express toward sexual harassment? Does it contradict or reinforce the formal policy? Do you share this attitude?

✔ What behaviors have you engaged in to create a workplace free of sexual harassment?

☞ *Record these on an easel chart.*

2. After about 45 minutes, reconvene the entire group and have each small group report the information recorded on their easel sheets:

• The ways they communicate their company's sexual harassment policy.

• The steps they can take to create a workplace free of sexual harassment.

3. After all the groups have reported, distribute copies of the **Establishing a Harassment-Free Workplace** worksheet and review any steps missed earlier in the exercise.

4. Explain that, legally, they have no choice: supervisors must act on sexual harassment or they put themselves and their organization at risk. Ignorance of the law is no excuse and does not hold up in court.

5. Form groups of 4 participants and have them discuss new behaviors they can use in order to be effective role models.

6. Conclude by inviting individuals to share what they intend to do when they return to their organization.

VARIATION

■ In *Step 5* of Activity 2, try to form groups of participants from the same organization so they can help support each other back on the job. Encourage them to meet periodically to share how their new strategies are working.

SEXUAL HARASSMENT POLICY

Directions: Complete the following open-ended sentences:

1. a.   My organization's sexual harassment policy is . . .

    b.   I don't know what my organization's sexual harassment policy is
         because . . .

2. As a manager or supervisor, I communicate my organization's sexual
   harassment policy by . . .

ESTABLISHING A HARASSMENT-FREE WORKPLACE

As a manager/supervisor:

1. Consider your own attitudes about sexual harassment and become informed yourself.

2. Don't participate in or condone behavior that is demeaning to women.

3. Talk with employees and peers about the subject.

4. Express strong disapproval of any kind of sexually harassing behavior.

5. Develop and enforce appropriate sanctions. You must take action even if the target asks you not to. Tell harassers the behavior is offensive to you as well as to the target.

6. Inform employees of their right to raise the issue of sexual harassment and the correct procedure to do so.

7. Educate and sensitize your subordinates to the issues through meetings and by example.

8. Be emotionally supportive of someone who tells you they have been sexually harassed and treat the incident seriously.

9. Have an open door policy, encouraging employees to report incidents—and always investigate the incidents.

10. Follow up with the victim to make sure the harassment has stopped and there are no reprisals.

11. Assume there may be sexual harassment in your organization and monitor the workplace environment through surveys, discussions with employees, etc.

12. Support the development of a strong harassment policy and the development of policies that deal with other kinds of discrimination.

©1995 Whole Person Press   210 W Michigan Duluth MN 55802   (800) 247-6789

17 CREATING A POLICY

This exercise, which works best with top level managers and committees who make or recommend policy, helps members of organizations create a strong, effective policy to prevent and handle sexual harassment.

GOALS

To develop or revise an organization's sexual harassment policy.

To understand the necessity of an effective policy.

To become familiar with the elements of a successful sexual harassment policy.

GROUP SIZE

Up to 25 participants.

TIME

2 hours.

MATERIALS

Magic markers; masking tape; easel and easel pad; **Creating a Sexual Harassment Policy** worksheets.

PROCESS

☞ *Before you start this session you should know if the organization has a policy. Ask participants to bring it with them if they do. Small companies may not have a policy at all, and some will have very ineffective ones. Make sure to get a clear agreement about the intent of the session with senior management.*

Activity 1: Why a Policy?

1. Introduce the exercise by explaining that this is a working session to create an effective sexual harassment policy for their organization.

2. Ask each participant to say why they think organizations today need a sexual harassment policy.

   ☞ *Record their answers on an easel chart. If someone does not think they need a policy, record their points on another easel chart and tell them you will respond to these points later.*

3. Summarize what they have said and add the following points if missed:

   • Having a policy shows management's commitment to eliminating discrimination and harassment and demonstrates their understanding of the problems.

   • It also gives employees information about what behavior will not be tolerated and puts them on notice that sexual harassment is not acceptable.

   • It encourages employees to make complaints known and provides guidance about how and where to complain.

   • It discourages harassment.

   • It reduces the company's liability in case of a lawsuit.

Activity 2: Elements of a Strong, Effective Policy

1. Distribute copies of the **Creating a Sexual Harassment Policy** worksheets and review the key elements to make sure all participants fully understand them.

2. Form small groups of 6-8 participants and provide the following instructions:

   ➤ If your organization currently has a policy, review it using the guidelines on the worksheet and develop recommendations for changes to make it more effective.

   ➤ If your organization currently does not have a policy, use the guidelines on the worksheet to create an effective policy outline.

   ➤ Record your recommendations on an easel chart.

   ➤ You have 1 hour.

3. After 1 hour, reconvene the entire group and have each group present the results of its work and answer questions other participants may have about their policy.

4. Post all the work on the wall and ask participants to walk around and place a check next to statements and changes they agree with and a question mark by those that they think need revision or explanation.

5. Reconvene the entire group and lead a discussion by identifying which items participants agreed on and which need further work.

6. Have participants agree on how they should finalize the policy.

☞ *Most groups assign a representative task group to work on the final policy. If you are meeting again, have the task group present it at that time or promise to mail a copy to all participants for final comments and approval before presenting it to senior management.*

7. Close with the following reminder:

- Policies are important, but without constant monitoring, feedback, and enforcement, policies are nothing more than words on a piece of paper.

- It is up to all of you to help make the policy work.

VARIATIONS

■ Have a senior manager or team attend the end of the session to hear the results and give feedback to the group.

■ Prior to the exercise, design and distribute a sexual harassment survey or conduct focus groups to gain information about specific problems the organization has encountered.

■ This exercise can be modified as a session to help representatives of many different organizations learn how to create an effective policy. In Activity 2, *Step 2* put representatives of the same or similar organizations in the same group and eliminate *Step 6*.

CREATING A
SEXUAL HARASSMENT POLICY

An effective sexual harassment policy should include:

1. A clear statement that sexual harassment and discrimination will not be tolerated.

2. The legal definition of sexual harassment.

3. A description of the different behaviors prohibited by the policy.

   A policy cannot describe every possible behavior, but it can give enough examples to become clear. Policies often include the following examples of inappropriate or illegal behavior:

   - Visual harassment: displaying sexual or nude pictures, cartoons, or calendars on company property; staring or leering at another's body.

   - Written harassment: E-mail messages that are sexual in nature; sexual or obscene letters, cards, or invitations.

   - Verbal harassment: sexual or obscene comments, jokes, innuendoes, or suggestions; spreading rumors about an employee's sex life; asking or telling about sexual fantasies, preferences, or history; negative or offensive comments; jokes or slurs about a person's gender, race, or sexual orientation.

   - Physical harassment: pinching or brushing up against another person in a suggestive way; touching yourself in a sexual manner in front of another person; physical violence or threat of violence; kissing, fondling or any other similar physical contact that another person finds unacceptable; sexual assault.

   - Blaming the victim: retaliation or punishment of the victim will not be tolerated.

4. Disciplinary actions.

   Highlight what actions will be taken for sexual harassment, up to and including dismissal.

CREATING A
SEXUAL HARASSMENT POLICY, continued

5. Guidelines on how to report harassment.

   Spell out how, when, and where employees can complain and outline the complaint process. Make sure to provide alternative places to file a complaint so targets do not have to go to their own supervisor. Allow employees to report to both women and men so they have a choice as to who they talk with about their complaint, informally and/or formally.

6. Organizational procedures.

   Form procedures to ensure that the complaint will be investigated in a prompt and confidential manner, that all parties involved will be treated fairly and receive all results of the investigation, and that there will be ongoing monitoring of the workplace environment and training sessions for managers and supervisors as well as employees.

18 SPEAKING UP

Participants use role playing to practice effective skills for confronting sexual harassment—works well in mixed-gender groups or when only women attend.

GOALS

To give participants tools to handle sexual harassment.

To develop nonviolent strategies to stop sexual harassment with direct action.

To empower women to demand respect as their rights.

To empower men to help confront sexual harassment.

GROUP SIZE

Up to 20 participants.

TIME

3 hours.

MATERIALS

Easel and easel pad; magic markers; masking tape; **Sexual Harassment Situations** worksheet; **Confrontation Strategies** worksheets; **Men as Allies** worksheet.

PROCESS

Activity 1: Personal Situations

1. Introduce the exercise with the following chalktalk:
   - Through socialization women have learned to respond to sexual harassment as helpless victims and to internalize their anger.
   - When women confront sexual harassment directly they challenge gender role socialization.
   - Most women are uncomfortable confronting harassment for many reasons, including fears of retaliation, of being negatively labeled, and of calling attention to themselves.

- Some women today are speaking up when sexually harassed, confronting it directly and immediately.

- When women confront sexual harassment they often leave the male harassers disoriented, confused, and no longer in control—they can potentially change the power dynamics.

- Many men are also reluctant to confront sexually harassing behavior, and some even feel pressure to join in with the "fun." Many men feel they are not supposed to break rank with the "Good Ol' Boys' Club."

- Some men, however, risk alienation when they recognize and confront unwelcome behavior. These men may lose some connection with the perpetrators, but they gain the respect of their female colleagues and other men who realize that harassment must end.

- Today we will have an opportunity to develop strategies to stop sexual harassment and practice using effective skills so you will be ready to take action the next time you find yourself a victim of or witness to sexual harassment.

2. Distribute copies of the **Sexual Harassment Situations** worksheet and provide the following instructions:

   ➤ Use the worksheet to describe sexual harassment you have encountered on the job, in school, church, or other organizations, or in public.

   ☞ *If there are men in the group, tell them they can also record any situations they have personally experienced, observed, or even participated in as a harasser.*

   ➤ Be specific when describing what the harasser(s) said or did and what your response was at the time.

   ➤ If you have encountered numerous situations, choose one or two examples for each place in which you experienced a harassment.

   ➤ You will have about 15 minutes.

3. After 15 minutes, call time and ask participants to place a star next to the situations they handled effectively and a check next to those they did not respond to well.

4. Form small groups of 6 participants and have them discuss their worksheets using the following questions:

   ☞ *Have them record their responses on an easel pad.*

   ✔ What kinds of responses were not effective?

✔ Did the ineffective responses confront the situation directly or indirectly?

✔ What kinds of responses, strategies, or techniques worked well to stop the harassment?

✔ Did the effective responses confront the situation directly or indirectly?

5. After about 30 minutes, reconvene the entire group and ask each group to report what they recorded, sharing first the ineffective techniques and then the effective tactics.

Activity 2: Effective Confrontation Techniques

1. Present the following chalktalk:

   ☞ *Use information participants developed in the previous activity to illustrate the points.*

   • For most of us who have been harassed, our objectives usually include:

     ○ First and foremost, to have the behavior stopped.

     ○ Second, to keep our job and maintain our effectiveness at work.

     ○ Third, to continue to have positive, respectful relationships with colleagues at work.

   • Some of you may have goals I have not included. Does anyone have any others to mention?

   • When you decide to take some action, use the following guidelines to increase your effectiveness:

     ☞ *Read the guidelines listed on the* **Confrontation Strategies** *worksheets and illustrate them with examples when necessary.*

   • Men can be very important allies in confronting sexual harassment. Some men may listen better to other men than to women. To be better allies to women in the fight to stop sexual harassment, use the following guidelines:

     ☞ *Read the guidelines listed on the* **Men as Allies** *worksheet and illustrate them with examples when necessary. If there are no male participants in this session, you do not need to cover this final chalktalk point.*

2. Distribute copies of the **Confrontation Strategies** worksheets (and **Men as Allies** worksheet if there are male participants) and tell

participants they will have an opportunity to practice these techniques in the next activity.

Activity 3: Role Play

1. Ask participants to take a few minutes to choose a situation from the first worksheet that they would like to practice handling more effectively in a role play.

2. Have participants take turns role-playing the situations they selected using the following process:

   ☞ *If the group size is larger than 12 participants, consider dividing the group in half for Step 2. If you have male participants, give them a chance to practice a situation in which they are allies. Or if they have been sexually harassed, they could also role play how to handle a similar situation.*

   a. Ask for a volunteer for the first role play and have her or him clearly describe the situation without going into its history in great detail.

   b. Select someone from the group to play the harasser(s) and allow time for him or her to ask questions about the harasser's behavior.

   c. Encourage the target (or ally) to use some of the confrontation skills from the worksheets.

   d. Start the role play by having the "harasser" behave in the unwelcome manner the target described in *Step a.*

   e. Stop when the confrontation has ended or when you have enough material for a discussion and ask the participants how they felt as they performed the role play.

   f. Have the target (or ally) give her- or himself feedback: What was done well? What needs improvement? etc.

   g. Ask the target (or ally) if she or he would like feedback from the group; if yes, invite the group to share what they believe was done well and what they think needs improvement.

   h. Replay any parts of the scene until the target (or ally) is satisfied that she or he can handle the situation in the future.

      ☞ *During the role play process, participants often realize how a target's passive response may encourage rather than stop further harassment. They may even become more comfortable speaking out about sexual harassment and reporting it after*

©1995 Whole Person Press   210 W Michigan Duluth MN 55802   (800) 247-6789

the practice session. Participants usually gain self confidence.

i. Repeat *Steps a–h* until each participant has had an opportunity to role-play their situation.

☞ *Make sure to emphasize that there is no right way to respond to sexual harassment and it is difficult for everyone to confront it. If a target still does not feel comfortable confronting sexual harassment after the role play, it is important not to push her. There are valid reasons not to speak up and the decision has to be the target's for she or he alone faces negative consequences.*

If a woman mentions violent behavior on the part of her harasser, such as life-threatening phone calls, encourage her not to confront him alone. Give her some options such as getting the support of coworkers or supervisors to confront him, filing a complaint, and—most importantly—reporting the behavior to the police.

3. Lead a discussion using the following questions:

✔ What did you learn from your role plays?

✔ What did you learn while observing others in their role plays?

4. End by encouraging targets to assert their right to respect in the workplace and men to show true respect for women by speaking up to other men.

VARIATION

■ If you would like to greatly enhance the learning process, videotape the role plays, then playback the videos and stop at key points for discussion. This adds about 10–15 minutes to each role play.

SEXUAL HARASSMENT SITUATIONS

Workplace:

School/College:

Church, medical, and other institutions (by ministers, doctors, etc.):

Public areas (bus, subway, street, elevators, stores, etc.):

Other:

CONFRONTATION STRATEGIES

1. Trust your instincts and admit to yourself a problem exists.

2. Don't delay—react immediately to the first incident (or a day or two after). If you have waited to take action, explain why you have said nothing in the past.

3. Know your rights and find out about the organization's policies and procedures as well as the sexual harassment law.

4. Say "no" directly and clearly.

5. Use assertive body language that demonstrates you are relaxed and confident: direct eye contact, movement toward the harasser, a strong, clear speaking voice. Do not smile or touch your harasser. Use "I" messages.

6. Avoid apologetic language or excuses.

7. Describe the harasser's behavior in specific terms, including what you find offensive about the behavior, its impact on you, and what behavior you would prefer. Do not use insults or slurs.

8. Use the "broken record" technique. Stay focused on your point and do not get sidetracked by irrelevant issues or labeling; ignore remarks and calmly repeat your point.

9. Don't keep it to yourself. Make your objection public. Tell trusting friends. Officially report it to supervisors, union representatives, and other persons in human resources or personnel departments.

10. Write down what happened. Keep a journal, a log of specific incidents, dates, times, places, witnesses, and the nature of the harassment. Save any offensive cards, letters, or photos. Do not destroy any notes or put any past personal information in the journal. Keep it in a safe place.

©1995 Whole Person Press   210 W Michigan Duluth MN 55802   (800) 247-6789

CONFRONTATION STRATEGIES, continued

11. Send a letter to the harasser explaining what behavior you object to, why you object to it, and what you want to have happen next (a good follow up to what you said in person). Keep a copy and send it by registered mail.

12. Act appropriately to the situation. Escalate your assertiveness if the behavior continues: Use stronger language and state what action you will take if the behavior doesn't stop.

13. Document your job performance to prepare for possible retaliation regarding your output.

14. File a police report if the behavior is criminal.

15. If the informal and/or formal company complaint process has not stopped the harassment, file a complaint with the Equal Employment Opportunity Commission or your state fair employment agency (if you work in a company with 15 or more employees).

16. Do not blame yourself. Get emotional support during this very stressful period and give yourself positive strokes for the strength you have shown.

17. Determine if there are others who have received similar offensive treatment from your harasser(s) and confront the harasser(s) or a supervisor as a group. Also identify any witnesses and enlist their support.

©1995 Whole Person Press   210 W Michigan Duluth MN 55802   (800) 247-6789

MEN AS ALLIES

1. Stop telling or laughing at sexist jokes or comments.

2. Ask questions about jokes or comments, such as "Why are you saying that about women?"

3. Don't smile at patronizing or insulting comments about women.

4. Don't leer, ogle, or make remarks to women in ways that make them uncomfortable. If you are unsure about what makes a woman uncomfortable, ask her.

5. Interrupt sexist or sexually harassing behavior by speaking up and saying you are personally offended by the harasser's attitude. Be assertive at first, not aggressive, but escalate the confrontation if the harasser does not respond appropriately.

6. Stop participating in male bonding activities that exclude or offend women.

7. Identify and discuss the issue when you witness sexual harassment.

8. Talk about sexism and sexual harassment with other men as part of your regular conversations.

9. Be open to examining your own sexism and sexist behavior.

10. Remember "no" means "no"—not "maybe;" never "yes."

©1995 Whole Person Press   210 W Michigan Duluth MN 55802   (800) 247-6789

19 WORKPLACE RESPONSIBILITIES

Using video vignettes of workplace harassment, participants explore how supervisors, witnesses, and targets can stop and prevent sexual harassment.

GOALS

To encourage group discussion on how to stop and prevent sexual harassment in the workplace.

To clarify the responsibilities of various persons to create a harassment-free workplace.

GROUP SIZE

Up to 30 participants.

TIME

1 hour.

MATERIALS

TV and VCR; **video vignettes**; **Sexual Harassment Responsibilities** worksheets.

> ☞ *Select 5 short scenes that illustrate sexual harassment from currently available videos. An excellent resource is Simmons Associates who have over twenty workplace vignettes on video to cover situations related to office environment, sales, manufacturing, etc. For more information, call (215) 862-3020.*

PROCESS

1. Explain that this exercise will explore how various people—targets, witnesses, and supervisors—are responsible to stop and prevent sexual harassment in the workplace.

2. Form 3 small groups and provide the following instructions:

   > ☞ *If possible, make sure the subgroup members are diverse in race, gender, age, and job positions.*

   ➤ I will show you a videotaped example of sexual harassment.

©1995 Whole Person Press   210 W Michigan Duluth MN 55802   (800) 247-6789

➤ Each group will then discuss the vignette from a different perspective, that of the harasser's supervisor, the target of the harassment, or a witness to the harassment.

☞ *Assign a different perspective to each group.*

➤ Discuss what options you have in dealing with the situation and the most effective way of handling it.

➤ You will have about 10 minutes to discuss the scenario and select a spokesperson to report your best choice as to how to handle the situation effectively.

3. Show the first vignette and allow the groups 10 minutes to discuss it.

4. Reconvene the entire group and ask a spokesperson from each small group to share their recommended course of action.

☞ *Start with the Supervisor group, then the Witness group, and finish with the Target group. Allow brief discussion and responses from facilitators (especially regarding legal issues).*

5. Give each group a new assignment (i.e., the Target group becomes the Witness group, etc.), play the second vignette, and repeat *Steps 3* and *4.*

6. Give each group a new assignment, show the third vignette, and repeat *Steps 3* and *4.*

7. Show the last two vignettes and lead a brief discussion of how to handle the situations with the entire group.

8. Distribute copies of the **Sexual Harassment Responsibilities** worksheets and give the following chalktalk:

• Through discussing the video vignettes, we have examined what supervisors, witnesses, and targets can do to prevent or stop sexual harassment.

• In many ways, those actions are really responsibilities—things we must feel obligated to do in order to prevent or stop sexual harassment.

• The worksheets you just received list those and many other responsibilities involved in preventing harassing behavior—including responsibilities of the harasser.

• Take time to read the worksheet and take the responsibility as a supervisor, witness, target—or harasser—to do what you can to make your workplace harassment-free.

VARIATIONS

■ If you are short on time, skip the small group activities and discuss all 5 video vignettes with the entire group.

■ Instead of using the generic video vignettes, make your own company video situations, role-play company situations, or use case histories prepared ahead of time that fit your company's typical cases of sexual harassment.

■ Have a civil rights specialist or company lawyer attend part of the exercise to address legal issues.

©1995 Whole Person Press   210 W Michigan Duluth MN 55802   (800) 247-6789

SEXUAL HARASSMENT RESPONSIBILITIES

Of the Supervisor

1. Understand your organization's harassment policy and the recommended procedures for handling sexual harassment complaints.

2. Be a role model by not making demeaning comments about gender, by speaking up when you hear any possibly demeaning remarks or see offensive behavior, and by being open to feedback from others about your own behavior.

3. Practice effective listening skills and listen actively when a person comes to you with a complaint. Be willing to hear the person's feelings and ask questions without attacking. Find out what action the employee wants to take and how the situation has affected her or his ability to do their job.

4. Be aware of what is happening in your department as well as in other areas of the organization. Practice walking around and tuning in to what is happening. Correct inappropriate behavior when you see it. Don't wait for a complaint.

5. Take every complaint seriously and investigate it, taking action immediately to stop and correct the inappropriate or offensive behavior, even if the person asks you not to (legally you must).

6. Respect the rights of all parties.

7. Document all your discussions and talk with all involved: the target, the alleged harasser, witnesses, others who might also been recipients of similar behavior.

8. Inform your supervisor and/or the appropriate company office of situations, your investigation, proposed actions, etc.

9. Take appropriate disciplinary action and follow the company's disciplinary procedures.

10. Follow up with the target to make sure there has been no retaliation since the complaint and that the behavior has stopped. You should also provide information on the actions you took.

11. Don't assume that no complaints means there are no problems in your workplace; many targets never complain.

12. Encourage constructive dialogue about sexism and sexual harassment. Offer periodic educational sessions about the topic. Post the sexual harassment policy where all employees will see it.

13. Have an open-door policy for sexual harassment problems.

©1995 Whole Person Press   210 W Michigan Duluth MN 55802   (800) 247-6789

SEXUAL HARASSMENT RESPONSIBILITIES

Of the Witness

1. When you witness sexual harassment or what you think might be taken as sexual harassment, talk to the targets and let them know you see what is happening and want to be supportive.

2. Speak up when you see offensive behavior and let the harassers know how you feel: "I find this behavior offensive and out of line for the workplace."

3. Do not tell or laugh at jokes that demean women or men.

4. Offer the following kinds of supportive behavior to the target, but let them decide what kinds of support they would like from you:

   • Express willingness to listen and talk about their experience, keeping these two points in mind:

      o Listen without judgment. Be open to hearing a target's experience. Never say something like: "I would have never stood there and taken that."

      o Listen to the feelings as well as the content of what targets say. Let them know you hear their feelings and do not question why they might have these feelings.

   • Volunteer to accompany targets when they confront harasser(s) or when they talk to the appropriate official about the complaint.

   • Offer to speak to the harasser yourself.

   • Help targets find resources and experts who can help.

   • Remind targets that what happened is not their fault.

5. Share your observations about sexual harassment with managers, peers, and others in the organization.

6. Participate in or initiate discussions about sexual harassment and sexism in your union, teams, and professional associations.

©1995 Whole Person Press   210 W Michigan Duluth MN 55802   (800) 247-6789

SEXUAL HARASSMENT RESPONSIBILITIES

Of the Target

1. Trust your feelings and recognize sexual harassment when it happens. Understand that it is not your fault and that it does not come with the job.

2. Learn about your legal rights and the organization's policies and procedures.

3. Talk to the harasser, telling him or her what you find offensive about their behavior, its impact on you, and what kind of behavior you want to receive in the future.

4. Put your objections to the harassment in writing; send a copy to the harasser and keep one for your files.

5. Tell others about the harassment, including supervisors, colleagues, Equal Employment Opportunity Commission counselors, union representatives, and friends.

6. Document all sexual harassment incidents or conversations about the incidents.

7. Document your job performance in case any retaliation regarding your work performance should occur.

8. Do not blame yourself and seek support.

9. Talk with others who may have been the recipients of similar treatment from your harasser(s) and if possible make a plan together. Also talk to any possible witnesses to enlist their support.

©1995 Whole Person Press   210 W Michigan Duluth MN 55802   (800) 247-6789

SEXUAL HARASSMENT RESPONSIBILITIES

Of the Harasser

1. Pay attention to nonverbal and verbal cues from others to what you do and say. If a response to your behavior seems negative, assume it is and stop the behavior.

2. If you think you may have offended someone, discuss it with her or him.

3. Assume that women, and many men, do not enjoy comments about their appearance, do not want to hear sexually-oriented jokes or comments, and do not appreciate being touched, stared at, or propositioned.

4. If someone tells you to stop how you're interacting with her or him, agree to stop and do not blame him or her or rationalize your behavior by talking about your good intentions.

5. If you are a supervisor or manager, do not assume that employees will be comfortable telling you if your behavior is offensive. Often employees may smile to hide that you have upset them because they are afraid of the power you hold over them as their supervisor.

6. Remember that sexual harassment is illegal. Recent court decisions have resulted in organizations and individuals paying large fines.

20 MANAGING INTIMACY

Participants discuss the risks and benefits of intimate relationships in the workplace and develop a sexual code of ethics for the organization—an excellent exercise for senior level managers and executives.

GOALS

To explore the risks and benefits of intimate relationships among coworkers.

To develop a sexual code of ethics that an organization or managers and employees can use as guidelines for relating as men and women.

GROUP SIZE

Up to 25 participants.

TIME

2 hours.

MATERIALS

Easel and easel pad; magic markers; masking tape;**Ethical Guidelines for Workplace Intimacy** worksheet.

PROCESS

Activity 1: Introduction to Managing Intimacy

1. Introduce the exercise with the following chalktalk:
   - Some of you may be confused about what constitutes appropriate behavior between men and women in the workplace.
   - Most organizations today want to eliminate sexual harassment among employees, but this does not mean eliminating sexuality from the workplace.
   - After all, sexuality is part of being human.
   - Many employees consider the workplace an acceptable and safe place to find a weekend date or even a life partner.
   - Intimate, close relationships—which may or may not include sexual feelings or behavior—naturally occur when people work together.

©1995 Whole Person Press   210 W Michigan Duluth MN 55802   (800) 247-6789

- In this exercise we will explore some of the issues involved in intimate relationships in the workplace, especially between men and women, and hopefully end up with a final product or rough draft of a sexual code of ethics to use in your department or organization.

2. Form groups of 4 participants and have them discuss the following questions:

    ✔ What are intimate work relationships? Are they different if we are talking about relationships between heterosexual colleagues of a single gender or about relationships between men and women or gay and lesbian colleagues?

    ☞ *The question attempts to make the point that "intimate" as used here does not necessarily indicate sexual relationships. If participants get confused, explain that many intimate work-place relationships are not sexual, although some may think they are.*

    ✔ Have you ever been attracted to someone in the workplace? How did you handle your feelings? What impact did it have on you? How do you think the relationship impacted others in the organization?

    ☞ *Make sure they understand that you are using "attraction" in the broad sense, not just in the physical sense.*

3. After about 20 minutes ask small group members to share any information about their own personal experiences that they think might be helpful to others.

4. Reconvene the entire group and summarize the information they just shared.

    ☞ *Make sure to mention that people respond differently. Some find being attracted to someone on the job or academic world to be stimulating and productive; for others it can be a distraction. In some cases it may cause resentment from others in the organization.*

Activity 2: Benefits and Negative Consequences

1. Have each group join another to create groups of 8 and assign the following task:

    ➤ Brainstorm a list of all the possible negative consequences of close relationships between women and men in the workplace and record it on an easel.

    ➤ Brainstorm a list of all the possible positive benefits of close relationships between women and men in the workplace and record it on an easel.

2. After 30 minutes, reconvene the entire group and have each group report and discuss the negative consequences they identified.

☞ *Usually they will mention resentment if a supervisor and subordinate have a close relationship (because it appears that the subordinate is exchanging personal or sexual resources for career advancement), gossip about the relationship, tension, etc.*

3. Have each group report and discuss the positive benefits they identified.

☞ *Usually they will mention improved teamwork and work group productivity.*

4. Lead a discussion about some of the issues connected with intimacy using the following questions:

✔ If men are fearful of either their own reactions or of receiving a sexual harassment complaint if they mentor a woman, how does this impact women's careers in the organization?

✔ Do we hold different standards for male/female relationships compared to same-gender relationships? For example, do you find yourself questioning what is going on when you see male and female colleagues having a long lunch or going on a business trip but not giving it a second thought if two men or two women do the same?

✔ What if two people want a personal relationship outside the workplace? Can they keep it a secret? Should they? What happens if the relationship ends badly?

✔ Can someone claim sexual harassment after they have been in an relationship with the person they accuse? How would you react to such a claim?

☞ *There are a number of cases where an employee has been subjected to harassment—even fired—after being in a relationship with another employee; often the harasser was also the target's boss.*

✔ Does your organization have any official or unofficial policies regarding coworker relationships? What are they?

Activity 3: Ethical Guidelines

1. Explain that the participants will now have an opportunity to develop a list of ethical guidelines for workplace relationships.

©1995 Whole Person Press   210 W Michigan Duluth MN 55802   (800) 247-6789

2. Distribute copies of the worksheet and ask participants to write down what they think would be excellent guidelines for conduct involving relationships in the workplace.

3. Reform the small groups of 8 participants and provide the following instructions:

   ➤ Share what you listed on your worksheets.

   ➤ As a group, develop a list of guidelines you all agree with.

   ➤ You have about 45 minutes.

   > ☞ *Facilitators should serve as consultants to the groups. Typical guidelines might include: Do not ask or pressure someone for dates after the other person has refused. It is not advisable for supervisors to date their subordinates; one of the parties should request a transfer to another division. We expect employees to have close relationships with others when it increases teamwork and productivity. Do not participate in rumors about coworker relationships.*

4. Reconvene the entire group and create a master list using the following process:

   a. Have a representative from each small group bring their list to the front of the room.

   b. Ask each to read their list and record the items on a master easel chart.

   c. If an item has already been recorded, place a star next to it each time it is mentioned by another group.

5. Lead a discussion of the items that were not agreed upon by all groups (the items not starred); eliminate some and keep others according to the consensus.

6. When a group consensus of the ethical guidelines has been reached, arrange for someone to word process it and provide copies to all the participants at a later date.

7. Lead a discussion about developing a plan to communicate the guidelines to employees that did not participate in the exercise.

VARIATIONS

■ Contact other companies and find out how they handle these issues and ask for copies of guidelines they have developed. Use this information during the session as an additional resource.

©1995 Whole Person Press   210 W Michigan Duluth MN 55802   (800) 247-6789

ETHICAL GUIDELINES FOR WORKPLACE INTIMACY

Directions: Create a list of guidelines for intimate relationships in the workplace.

1.

2.

3.

4.

5.

6.

7.

8.

9.

10.

©1995 Whole Person Press   210 W Michigan Duluth MN 55802   (800) 247-6789

TRAINER'S NOTES

Resources

READING LIST

Backhouse, Connie, and Leah Cohen. *Sexual Harassment on the Job: How To Avoid the Working Woman's Nightmare*. Englewood Cliffs, N.J.: Prentice Hall, 1981.

Barreca, Regina. *They Used to Call Me Snow White . . . But I Drifted*. New York: Penguin Books, 1991.

Barry, Kathleen. *Female Sexual Slavery*. Englewood Cliffs, N.J.: Prentice Hall, 1981.

Bravo, Ellen, and Ellen Cassedy. *The 9 to 5 Guide to Combating Sexual Harassment: Candid Advice from 9 to 5*. The National Association of Working Women. New York: John Wiley & Sons, 1992.

Coverdale-Sumrall, Amber, and Dena Taylor, eds. *Sexual Harassment: Women Speak Out*. Freedom, Calif.: Crossing Press, 1992.

Dworkin, Andrea. *Letters From a War Zone: Writings, 1976–1989*. New York: E. P. Dutton, 1989.

Dziech, Billie Wright and Linda Weiner. *The Lecherous Professor: Sexual Harassment on Campus*. Chicago: University of Illinois Press, 1990.

Eskenazi, Martin, and David Gallen. *Sexual Harassment: Know Your Rights!* New York: Carroll & Graff, 1992.

Farley, Lin. *Sexual Shakedown: The Sexual Harassment of Women on the Job*. New York: McGraw-Hill, 1978.

Gomez-Preston, Cherly. *When No Means No*. New York: Birch Lane Press, 1993.

Gutek, Barbara. *Sex and the Workplace: The Impact of Sexual Behavior and Harassment on Women, Men, and Organizations*. San Francisco: Jossey-Bass, 1985.

Hardesty, Sarah and Nehama Jacobs. *Success and Betrayal: The Crisis of Women in Corporate America*. New York: Simon & Schuster, 1986.

Langelan, Martha. *Back Off*. New York: Fireside Press, 1993.

Lindemann, B. and D. Kadue. *Sexual Harassment in Employment Law*. Washington, DC: BNA, Inc., 1992.

McAllister, Pam. *You Can't Kill the Spirit.* Philadelphia: New Society Publishers, 1988.

——*This River of Courage: Generations of Women's Resistance and Action.* Philadelphia: New Society Publishers, 1991.

McCann, Nancy Dodd, and Thomas A. McGinn. *Harassed: 100 Women Define Inappropriate Behavior in the Workplace.* Homewood, Ill.: Business One Irwin, 1992.

MacKinnon, Catharine A. *Sexual Harassment of Working Women.* New Haven: Yale University Press, 1979.

Mainiero, Lisa. Office Romance: Love, Power and Sex in the Workplace. New York: Rawson Associates, 1989.

Morris, Celia. *Bearing Witness.* Boston: Little, Brown & Co., 1994.

Morrison,Toni, ed. *Race-ing Justice, En-gendering Power: Essays on Anita Hill, Clarence Thomas, and the Construction of Social Reality.* New York: Pantheon Books, 1992.

Paludi, Michele A., ed. *Ivory Power: Sexual Harassment on Campus.* Albany: State University of New York Press, 1990.

Paludi, Michele A. and Richard Barickman. *Academic and Workplace Harassment: A Resource Manual.* Albany: State University of New York Press, 1991.

Petrocelli, William and Barbara Kate Repa. *Sexual Harassment on the Job: A Step-By-Step Guide for Working Women.* Berkeley, Calif.: Nola Press, 1992.

Siegal, Deborah L. *Sexual Harassment: Research and Resources.* New York: National Council for Research on Women, 1991.

Van Hyning, Memory. *Crossed Signals.* Los Angeles: Infotrend Press, 1993.

Wagner, Ellen J. *Sexual Harassment in the Workplace: How to Prevent, Investigate, and Resolve Problems in Your Organization.* New York: AMACOM, 1992.

Webb, Susan L. *Step Forward, Sexual Harassment in the Workplace: What You Need to Know.* New York: Mastermedia, 1991.

Wise, Sue, and Liz Stanley. *Georgie Porgie: Sexual Harassment in Everyday Life.* New York: Pandora, 1987.

©1995 Whole Person Press   210 W Michigan Duluth MN 55802   (800) 247-6789

HOW TO USE THIS BOOK
MOST EFFECTIVELY

THE CONCEPT OF EXPERIENTIAL LEARNING

As you will notice with just a cursory glance through this volume, these educational experiences actively involve participants in the learning process. Why? Because when you draw on the resources of the group in your presentations, you empower people.

Every session in this book balances didactic information and group participation. Experiential training concentrates on developing awareness and understanding plus building skills that can be used at home and on the job. This model helps participants become involved and therefore makes it more likely they will assume responsibility for their own learning.

Each exercise is designed to create opportunities for participants to interact with the concepts and each other in meaningful ways. The lecture method is replaced with succinct chalktalks and facilitative questions that guide people to discover their own answers. The authority of the trainer is transformed into the authority of the individual's inner wisdom.

THE TRAINER'S CHALLENGE

For many teachers, giving up the authority implicit in the typical lecture format is a risky proposition. Trainers are often afraid that they won't be perceived as an expert, so they are tempted to lecture, entertain and keep the focus on themselves. Yet, if your goal is truly to help people change, information is not enough. Praise from your audience is not enough. What really counts are the discoveries participants make about their own patterns and the choices they make to manage their lives more effectively.

Remember, as a trainer, you are not presenting a paper at a conference. You are engaging an audience in an educational process. Your task is to appeal to people with different learning styles, using a wide variety of strategies to get them involved. In whole person learning, the questions are as important as the content.

©1995 Whole Person Press   210 W Michigan Duluth MN 55802   (800) 247-6789

THE TEACHING STRATEGIES

These exercises help you involve people in the process of reflecting, prioritizing, sorting, and planning for change by using the following strategies.

1. **Activating participants' internal wisdom**: This is best accomplished by asking questions that help people come up with answers that are right for them, rather than by giving them your "right answers."

2. **Helping people make choices**: These exercises assist people to sort out their own values and priorities, helping them to explore their beliefs and assumptions and encouraging them to alter their lives in ways that they choose, based on their own sense of rhythm and timing.

3. **Activating the group's resources**: These exercises take the dynamic of the group seriously. The first five minutes are the key! They help you get people involved with each other right off the bat, and let you use and work with the energy of the group—the laughter, the group norms, the embarrassment, the competition.

4. **Fostering interpersonal support**: With these exercises you capitalize on the rich variety of experiences and insights among your participants. And you capitalize on the power of their support for each other. Interaction builds trust, helps people consider new options, and offers support for change. For many people this chance to compare notes with others is the most powerful part of the session.

THE RHYTHM OF EACH SESSION

To accomplish these teaching objectives each exercise is designed to include a rhythmic sequence of activities with enough change of pace to keep the group's involvement and energy high. Most exercises include:

A warm-up—An introductory activity that gets people involved with each other around the subject in an energetic and playful manner.

A chalktalk—A brief introduction to the session's main concepts.

Personal reflection—Questions to help each participant test the concepts against their own life experiences in order to determine which ideas make sense to them.

Inductive summary—A pooling of the group's observations and insights.

©1995 Whole Person Press   210 W Michigan Duluth MN 55802   (800) 247-6789

Planning/commitment—The bottom line in training. Everyone should leave the session with at least one clear idea about what they will do next.

THE FORMAT

The format of this book is designed for easy use. Every exercise is described completely, including goals, group size, time, materials needed, step-by-step process instructions, and variations. The format employs the following symbols to help indicate specific items:

☞ *Special instructions for the trainer are set in italics and preceded by a pointing hand.*

✔ Questions to ask participants are preceded by a check.

➤ Instructions for group activities are indicated by an arrow.

● Chalktalk (mini-lecture) notes and sentence-completion fragments are preceded by a bullet.

Time: The time frame provided at the beginning of each exercise and times given for various activities within the process are only guidelines— suggestions to help you organize and schedule a successful workshop. Feel free to adapt the times as you feel necessary.

Worksheets: Many of the exercises include worksheets for participants to complete. The worksheets can be found immediately following the exercises in which they are to be used. Make certain you photocopy enough worksheets for all your participants prior to conducting an exercise. (8 1/2" x 11" photocopy masters for this book are also available from Whole Person Associates.)

Chalktalks: Most of the exercises include chalktalk notes—bulleted lists of information that help introduce an exercise or provide vital information on its topic. These notes provide a framework to help you develop a complete mini-lecture of your own.

TIPS FOR USING THESE EXERCISES MOST EFFECTIVELY

1. **Tailor your process to the group**: Read the objectives for each exercise and carefully choose those you will use. Remember, these exercises are more than fun and games. Each has a clear purpose.

   Decide what is appropriate based on the setting, the time available, the purpose and the participants' style and comfort level. Exercises should be specifically selected for a particular organization and should be tailored to that organization's style and culture. What will work well in one situation may not work as effectively in another. Feel free to adapt exercises as you deem necessary.

2. **Pay attention to the timing**: In your planning, anticipate the needs and rhythm of the group. At the first session you'll need more time for setting the ground rules and getting acquainted. In later sessions, as people get to know each other better you'll need to allocate more time for the discussion segments.

Every group goes through predictable (and unpredictable!) cycles. Anticipate peak times and down times during the day and plan for changing the pace as needed to restore energy and enthusiasm.

3. **Prepare yourself thoroughly for each session**: Good teaching is built on examples and anecdotes. In order to make the material come alive for you and for others, you will need to carefully work through each session and personalize each segment with your own examples and stories. You can do this in a number of ways:

- Read the detailed exercise outline thoroughly. Be sure you understand the basic concepts and processes for the session. Answer all worksheet questions for yourself. This will help you anticipate difficulties and will provide you with lively personal examples.

- Reread the chalktalk notes one point at a time. Translate the ideas into your own words. Personalize each concept with carefully chosen examples that you think will fit the group's needs.

- Add diagrams, cartoons, newspaper articles—whatever relevant information you come across during your preparation.

- Relax. Take a few minutes by yourself before you begin each session so that you are centered and focused.

4. **Make the environment work for you**: The room makes a very important contribution to the atmosphere. The best location has soft lighting, comfortable chairs, is neither too big nor too small, and has privacy to prevent interruptions that would distract the group. If you must meet in a room that's too large, keep the group together. Don't let people spread out all over—distance breeds isolation.

Banked auditoriums with fixed seats are workable, but not recommended. The inflexibility of the seating makes movement exercises and small group gatherings more difficult.

Encourage participants to sit in a circle. This creates the most successful setting since it provides an ideal forum for verbal and nonverbal communication and offers an atmosphere of inclusion.

©1995 Whole Person Press   210 W Michigan Duluth MN 55802   (800) 247-6789

You will want to have a chalkboard or sheets of newsprint (or both!) available for your use at all times.

Don't expect anyone else to set up the room for you. Get there early and, if necessary, set it up yourself.

5. **Establish a supportive atmosphere**: Participants in your sessions must feel safe enough to examine their attitudes and beliefs and to change some of them. A trainer open to listening to what all participants say creates an atmosphere of security.

Always restate a participant's comment or question before you respond. Summarizing what you heard affirms the person and shows your audience that you are listening and taking them seriously.

Begin the workshop with a discussion of guidelines for the session. This helps alleviate anxiety and sets a positive tone. Suggestions include: attend regularly and be on time, listen to each other carefully, and respect confidentiality.

6. **Carefully plan the small group discussions**: For most discussions, groups of four to six are optimal. Timing will be a problem if some groups have three people and others have eight. So try to keep groups the same size as indicated in the instructions.

In many exercises your leader notes tell you how to divide the participants into small groups. In others the "how to" is left up to you.

If some people don't participate (or even leave the room during group sharing time) don't panic. Don't drop the group experience because a few people feel uncomfortable. For many people the small group discussions are the most valuable part of the session.

7. **Grow from this experience yourself**: Try to learn the most you can from every event. Don't be afraid to share yourself. You are a leader/participant! Don't be discouraged if each session does not go exactly as you had expected. Turn disasters into opportunities. When something does not go well, laugh! When all else fails, start asking questions.

Plan to have fun! The processes in these exercises are designed so that you have a chance to listen as well as talk. The whole experience does not depend on you. Open your eyes and your ears, you'll learn something too!

©1995 Whole Person Press   210 W Michigan Duluth MN 55802   (800) 247-6789

Whole Person Associates
Resources

All printed, audio, and video resources developed by Whole Person Associates are designed to address the whole person—physical, emotional, mental, spiritual, and social. On the next pages, trainers will find a wide array of resources that offer ready-to-use ideas and concepts they can add to their programs.

GROUP PROCESS RESOURCES

All of the exercises in these group process resources encourage interaction between the leader and participants, as well as among the participants. Each exercise includes everything needed to present a meaningful program.

WORKING WITH WOMEN'S GROUPS
Volumes 1 & 2
Louise Yolton Eberhardt

The two volumes of **Working with Women's Groups** have been completely revised and updated. **Volume 1** explores consciousness raising, self-discovery, and assertiveness training. **Volume 2** looks at sexuality issues, women of color, and leadership skills training.

☐ **Working with Women's Groups**
   Volumes 1 & 2 / $24.95 per volume

WORKING WITH MEN'S GROUPS
Roger Karsk and Bill Thomas

Working with Men's Groups has been updated to reflect the reality of men's lives in the 1990s. Each exercise follows a structured pattern to help trainers develop either one-time workshops or ongoing groups that explore men's issues in four key areas: self-discovery, consciousness raising, intimacy, and parenting.

☐ **Working with Men's Groups / $24.95**

WORKSHEET MASTERS
Complete packages of (8 1/2" x 11") photocopy masters are available for **Working with Women's Groups** and **Working with Men's Groups**. Use the masters to conveniently duplicate handouts for each participant.

☐ **Worksheet Masters / $9.95 per volume**

To order, call toll free   (800) 247-6789

WORKING WITH GROUPS IN THE WORKPLACE

This new collection addresses the special needs and concerns of trainers in the workplace. As the work force changes, EAP counselors, education departments, and management are being called on to guide and support their employees who face the challenges of a more diverse workplace.

BRIDGING THE GENDER GAP
Louise Yolton Eberhardt

Bridging the Gender Gap contains a wealth of exercises for the trainer to use with men and women who work as colleagues. These activities will also be useful in gender role awareness groups, diversity training, couples workshops, college classes, and youth seminars.

❑ **Bridging the Gender Gap / $24.95**

CONFRONTING SEXUAL HARASSMENT
Louise Yolton Eberhardt

Confronting Sexual Harassment presents exercises that trainers can safely use with groups to constructively explore the issues of sexual harassment, look at the underlying causes, understand the law, motivate men to become allies, and empower women to speak up.

❑ **Confronting Sexual Harassment / $24.95**

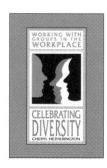

CELEBRATING DIVERSITY
Cheryl Hetherington

Celebrating Diversity helps people confront and question the beliefs, prejudices, and fears that can separate them from others. Carefully written exercises help trainers present these sensitive issues in the workplace as well as in educational settings.

❑ **Celebrating Diversity / $24.95**

WORKSHEET MASTERS
Complete packages of (8 1/2" x 11") photocopy masters are available for all books in the **Working with Groups in the Workplace** series.

❑ **Worksheet Masters / $9.95 per volume**

To order, call toll free   (800) 247-6789

STRESS AND WELLNESS ANNOTATED GUIDES

From worksite health promotion to life-style research to family stress, these authoritative reviews of classic and contemporary information sources will help you locate the resources you need for planning workshops, classes, program proposals, or presentations on stress and wellness.

STRESS RESOURCES
An annotated guide to essential books, periodicals, A-V materials and teaching tools about stress for trainers, consultants, counselors, educators and health professionals

Selected and reviewed by Jim Polidora, Ph.D.

Jim Polidora reviews the best current and classic, popular and scientific literature in every area of stress management. Over 500 annotations are arranged topically for easy reference.

Each of the fifteen chapters includes reviews of books and audiovisual resources. Special sections feature textbooks, catalogs, journals, newsletters, and stress-related organizations.

❑ **Stress Resources / $34.95**

WELLNESS RESOURCES
An annotated guide to essential books, periodicals, A-V materials and teaching tools about wellness for trainers, consultants, counselors, educators and health professionals

Selected and reviewed by Jim Polidora, Ph.D.

This first comprehensive guide to wellness resources is packed with descriptions of over 500 of the best current and classic books, audiotapes, videotapes, journals, newsletters, and catalogs.

The fifteen chapters of reading and viewing suggestions in **Wellness Resources** make workshop or program planning a breeze.

❑ **Wellness Resources / $34.95**

To order, call toll free   (800) 247-6789

STRUCTURED EXERCISES IN STRESS MANAGEMENT

Nancy Loving Tubesing, EdD, and Donald A. Tubesing, PhD, Editors

Each book in this four-volume series contains 36 ready-to-use teaching modules that involve the participant—as a whole person—in learning how to manage stress more effectively.

Each volume brims with practical ideas that mix and match allowing trainers to develop new programs for varied settings, audiences, and time frames. Each volume contains **Icebreakers, Stress Assessments, Management Strategies, Skill Builders, Action Planners, Closing Processes,** and **Group Energizers**.

❑ **Stress 8 1/2" x 11" Loose-Leaf Edition—Volume 1-4 / $54.95 each**
❑ **Stress 6" x 9" Softcover Edition—Volume 1-4 / $29.95 each**

STRUCTURED EXERCISES IN WELLNESS PROMOTION

Nancy Loving Tubesing, EdD, and Donald A. Tubesing, PhD, Editors

Each of the four volumes in this innovative series includes 36 experiential learning activities that focus on whole person health—body, mind, spirit, emotions, relationships, and life-style.

Icebreakers, Wellness Explorations, Self-Care Strategies, Action Planners, Closings, and **Group Energizers** are all ready-to-go—including reproducible worksheets, scripts, and chalktalk outlines—for the busy professional who wants to develop unique wellness programs without spending hours in preparation.

❑ **Wellness 8 1/2" x 11" Loose-Leaf Edition—Volume 1-4 / $54.95 each**
❑ **Wellness 6" x 9" Softcover Edition—Volume 1-4 / $29.95 each**

WORKSHEET MASTERS

Complete packages of (8 1/2" x 11") photocopy masters are available for all **Structured Exercises in Stress Management** and **Structured Exercises in Wellness Promotion**. Use the masters to conveniently duplicate handouts for each participant.

❑ **Worksheet Masters / $9.95 per volume**

To order, call toll free   (800) 247-6789

RELAXATION AUDIOTAPES

Perhaps you're an old hand at relaxation, looking for new ideas. Or maybe you're a beginner, just testing the waters. Whatever your relaxation needs, Whole Person audiotapes provide a whole family of options for reducing physical and mental stress.

Techniques range from simple breathing and stretching exercises to classic autogenic and progressive relaxation sequences, guided meditations, and whimsical daydreams. All are carefully crafted to promote whole person relaxation—body, mind, and spirit.

If you're looking for an extended relaxation experience (20 minutes or more), try a tape from the Sensational Relaxation, Guided Imagery, or Wilderness Daydreams groups. For quick R&R breaks (5–10 minutes), try a Stress Breaks, Daydreams or Mini-Meditations collections. All of our tapes feature male and female narrators.

Audiotapes are available for $11.95 each.
Call for generous quantity discounts.

SENSATIONAL RELAXATION—$11.95 each
When stress piles up, it becomes a heavy load both physically and emotionally. These full-length relaxation experiences will teach you techniques that can be used whenever you feel that stress is getting out of control. Choose one you like and repeat it daily until it becomes second nature, then recall that technique whenever you need it or try a new one every day.

- ❑ **Countdown to Relaxation /** Countdown 19:00, Staircase 19:00
- ❑ **Daybreak / Sundown /** Daybreak 22:00, Sundown 22:00
- ❑ **Take a Deep Breath /** Breathing for Relaxation 17:00, Magic Ball 17:00
- ❑ **Relax . . . Let Go . . . Relax /** Revitalization 27:00, Relaxation 28:00
- ❑ **StressRelease /** Quick Tension Relievers 22:00,Progressive Relaxation 20:00
- ❑ **Warm and Heavy /** Warm 24:00, Heavy 23:00

STRESS BREAKS—$11.95 each
Do you need a short energy booster or a quick stress reliever? If you don't know what type of relaxation you like, or if you are new to guided relaxation techniques, try one of our Stress Breaks for a quick refocusing or change of pace any time of the day.

- ❑ **BreakTime /** Solar Power 8:00, Belly Breathing 9:00, Fortune Cookie 9:00, Mother Earth 11:00, Big Yawn 5:00, Affirmation 11:00
- ❑ **Natural Tranquilizers /** Clear the Deck 10:00, Body Scan 10:00, 99 Countdown 10:00, Calm Down 9:00, Soothing Colors 11:00, Breathe Ten 9:00

To order, call toll free   (800) 247-6789

DAYDREAMS—$11.95 each

Escape from the stress around you with guided tours to beautiful places. The quick escapes in our Daydreams tapes will lead your imagination away from your everyday cares so you can resume your tasks relaxed and comforted.

- ❑ **Daydreams 1: Getaways /** Cabin Retreat 11:00, Night Sky 10:00, Hot Spring 7:00, Mountain View 8:00, Superior Sail 8:00
- ❑ **Daydreams 2: Peaceful Places /** Ocean Tides 11:00, City Park 10:00, Hammock 8:00, Meadow 11:00
- ❑ **Daydreams 3: Relaxing Retreats /** Melting Candle 5:00, Tropical Paradise 10:00, Sanctuary 7:00, Floating Clouds 5:00, Seasons 9:00, Beach Tides 9:00

GUIDED MEDITATION—$11.95 each

Take a step beyond relaxation. The imagery in our full-length meditations will help you discover your strengths, find healing, make positive life changes, and recognize your inner wisdom.

- ❑ **Inner Healing /** Inner Healing 20:00, Peace with Pain 20:00
- ❑ **Personal Empowering /** My Gifts 22:00, Hidden Strengths 21:00
- ❑ **Healthy Balancing /** Inner Harmony 20:00, Regaining Equilibrium 20:00
- ❑ **Spiritual Centering /** Spiritual Centering 20:00 (male and female narration)

WILDERNESS DAYDREAMS—$11.95 each

Discover the healing power of nature with the four tapes in our Wilderness Daydreams series. The eight special journeys will transport you from your harried, stressful surroundings to the peaceful serenity of words and water.

- ❑ **Canoe / Rain /** Canoe 19:00, Rain 22:00
- ❑ **Island / Spring /** Island 19:00, Spring 19:00
- ❑ **Campfire / Stream /** Campfire 17:00, Stream 19:00
- ❑ **Sailboat / Pond /** Sailboat 25:00, Pond 25:00

MINI-MEDITATIONS—$11.95 each

These brief guided visualizations begin by focusing your breathing and uncluttering your mind, so that you can concentrate on a sequence of sensory images that promote relaxation, centering, healing, growth, and spiritual awareness.

- ❑ **Healing Visions /** Rocking Chair 5:00, Pine Forest 8:00, Long Lost Confidant 10:00, Caterpillar to Butterfly 7:00, Superpowers 9:00, Tornado 8:00
- ❑ **Refreshing Journeys /** 1 to 10 10:00, Thoughts Library 11:00, Visualizing Change 6:00, Magic Carpet 9:00, Pond of Love 9:00, Cruise 9:00

MUSIC ONLY—$11.95 each

No relaxation program would be complete without relaxing melodies that can be played as background to a prepared script or that can be enjoyed as you practice a technique you have already learned. Steven Eckels composed his melodies specifically for relaxation. These "musical prayers for healing" will calm your body, mind, and spirit.

- ❑ **Tranquility /** Awakening 20:00, Repose 20:00
- ❑ **Harmony /** Waves of Light 30:00, Rising Mist 10:00, Frankincense 10:00, Angelica 10:00
- ❑ **Serenity /** Radiance 20:00, Quiessence 10:00, Evanesence 10:00

To order, call toll free   (800) 247-6789

RELAXATION RESOURCES

Many trainers and workshop leaders have discovered the benefits of relaxation and visualization in healing the body, mind, and spirit.

30 SCRIPTS FOR RELAXATION, IMAGERY, AND INNER HEALING
Julie Lusk

The relaxation scripts, creative visualizations and guided meditations in these volumes were created by experts in the field of guided imagery. Julie Lusk collected their best and most effective scripts to help novices get started and experienced leaders expand their repertoire. Both volumes include information on how to use the scripts, suggestions for tailoring them to specific needs and audiences, and information on how to successfully incorporate guided imagery into existing programs.

❑ **30 Scripts**
   Volume 1 & 2 / $19.95 each

GUIDED IMAGERY FOR GROUPS
Andrew Schwartz

Ideal for courses, workshops, team building, and personal stress management, this comprehensive resource includes scripts for 50 thematic visualizations that promote calming, centering, creativity, congruence, clarity, coping, and connectedness. Detailed instructions for using relaxation techniques and guided images in group settings allow educators at all levels, in any setting, to help people tap into the healing and creative powers of imagery.

❑ **Guided Imagery for Groups / $24.95**

INQUIRE WITHIN
Andrew Schwartz

Use visualization to help people make positive changes in their life. The 24 visualization experiences in **Inquire Within** will help participants enhance their creativity, heal inner pain, learn to relax, and deal with conflict. Each visualization includes questions at the end of the process that encourage deeper reflection and a better understanding of the exercise and the response it evokes.

❑ **Inquire Within / $19.95**

To order, call toll free   (800) 247-6789

PLAYFUL ACTIVITIES FOR POWERFUL PRESENTATIONS
Bruce Williamson

Spice up presentations with healthy laughter. The 40 creative energizers in *Playful Activities for Powerful Presentations* will enhance learning, stimulate communication, promote teamwork, and reduce resistance to group interaction.

This potent but light-hearted resource will make presentations on any topic more powerful and productive.

❑ Playful Activities for Powerful Presentations $19.95

WORKING WITH GROUPS FROM DYSFUNCTIONAL FAMILIES
Cheryl Hetherington

Even the healthiest family can be dysfunctional at times, making everyone vulnerable to the pain of difficult family relationships.

This collection of 29 proven group activities is designed to heal the pain that results from living in a dysfunctional family. With these exercises leaders can promote healing, build self-esteem, encourage sharing, and help participants acknowledge their feelings.

❑ Working with Groups from Dysfunctional Families / $24.95

WORKSHEET MASTERS
A complete package of (8 1/2" x 11") photocopy masters is available for **Working with Groups from Dysfunctional Families**. Use the masters to conveniently duplicate handouts for each participant.
❑ Worksheet Masters / $9.95 per volume

To order, call toll free   (800) 247-6789

VIDEO RESOURCES

These video-based workshops use the power of professionally produced videotapes as a starting point. Then they build on the experience with printed guides chock-full of suggestions, group processes, and personal growth exercises that build sessions participants will remember!

MAKING HEALTHY CHOICES

Making Healthy Choices, a complete six-session, video-based course on healthy living, encourages people to begin making the choices, large and small, that promote wellness in all areas of their lives. Save $95.00 by purchasing the complete set or select individual sessions.

- ❑ **MAKING HEALTHY CHOICES SET / $474.00**
- ❑ **Healthy Lifestyle / $95.00**
- ❑ **Healthy Eating / $95.00**
- ❑ **Healthy Exercise / $95.00**
- ❑ **Healthy Stress / $95.00**
- ❑ **Healthy Relationships / $95.00**
- ❑ **Healthy Change / $95.00**

MANAGING JOB STRESS

Managing Job Stress, a comprehensive six-session stress management course, takes aim at a universal problem: work-related stress. Each session emphasizes positive responses to the challenges of on-the-job stress. Save $95.00 by purchasing the entire set or select individual sessions.

- ❑ **MANAGING JOB STRESS SET / $474.00**
- ❑ **Handling Workplace Pressure / $95.00**
- ❑ **Clarifying Roles and Expectations / $95.00**
- ❑ **Controlling the Workload / $95.00**
- ❑ **Managing People Pressures / $95.00**
- ❑ **Surviving the Changing Workplace / $95.00**
- ❑ **Balancing Work and Home / $95.00**

MANAGE IT!

Manage It! is an innovative six-part video-based series that helps participants develop management skills for handling stress. Participants learn new coping skills and practice a relaxation technique for immediate on-the-spot stress relief. Save $95.00 by purchasing the entire set or select individual sessions.

- ❑ **MANAGE IT! SET / $474.00**
- ❑ **Stress Traps / $95.00**
- ❑ **Stress Overload / $95.00**
- ❑ **Interpersonal Conflict / $95.00**
- ❑ **Addictive Patterns / $95.00**
- ❑ **Job Stress / $95.00**
- ❑ **Survival Skills / $95.00**

To order, call toll free   (800) 247-6789